BUSY!

The working mum's guide
to confidently walking
life's tightrope

MARIA ANDREAS NEWMAN

Published in 2022 by Discover Your Bounce Publishing

www.discoveryourbouncepublishing.com

ISBN 978-1-914428-07-4

Page design and typesetting by Discover Your Bounce Publishing

DEDICATION

I dedicate this book to my loving and supportive husband Simon and my inspiring and formidable children, Lea and Louka.

This book is also dedicated to all mums. You're doing your best and that is good enough.

CONTENTS

⟩ FOREWORD ⟨

I've had the pleasure of knowing Maria for the past four years and am truly honoured to call her both a friend and mentor. We are both members of a group called Freelance Mum in Bristol and Maria is one of the people who truly epitomises what it is to be a 'freelance mum'. Not only is she raising two clever, sweet and inquisitive children but she has also used that same gentle, motherly nature to form a business.

Maria has such a kind, gentle way of encouraging women to become who they were meant to be, and I am just one of the many recipients of her unique course. I became a mum in 2017 and found, like many other mums, that I became distracted from taking care of myself and remembering my own life goals. It's hard balancing parenting and a career, which is why many of us feel unable to do both or feel as if we're failing when we do.

As mums we often forget to prioritise ourselves, putting ourselves at the bottom of the pile as we know we can keep running on fumes when our energy is spent elsewhere. We forget our career and life goals, our wants and wishes for our lives, as just trying to keep going becomes the status quo.

Fortunately, Maria also knows this feeling first hand and decided to do something to help us mums who need a bit of support to find ourselves again. This desire has led Maria to create a course you can follow while you're busy looking after your children, and all the information you need is in this very book!

While it's true that there are other books you could read about following your dreams and meeting challenges, I can tell you that you won't find another book that feels like the author is your friend and is holding your trembling hand throughout this process.

If you're someone who is looking for a little encouragement in your life, career or need to make some big decisions about your future, this is the book for you.

After reading it I immediately recommended it to a number of my friends who have expressed the need for a book just like this.

Maria is a warm hug of a person, and this is exactly how this book feels.

Rachel Walker Mason

BCA Bestselling Author, Songwriter and 2020 Woman Of The Year

INTRODUCTION

Well, hello. I'm so pleased you decided to invest in yourself and read this book. Let me introduce myself properly. My name is Maria, otherwise known as Mummy on a Break and the founder of The Busy Working Mums Club.

I'm an ordinary mum, just like you, trying to live my best life. I know that sounds like a cliché but it's true. So many women. So many mums. They're just going through the motions of life thinking that is what life should be. Thinking everything is okay so there's no need to do anything differently.

Well, that's not true. You deserve better than okay. You deserve great. You deserve to be making your dreams a reality.

Yes, I know that's what they all say. So, if they're all saying it then why are we all not living our best lives?

The truth is it's easier to just sit in okay. Making your dreams come true takes effort and focus. As well as the determination to make it happen.

But once you start, once you get the wheels in motion, there will be no stopping you. You will find your momentum and before you know it your life will be everything you want it to be.

3

But what is going to trigger you to take that leap of faith and make a start today? To commit to making a change?

What you don't need to wait for is a tragedy or major drama in your life.

What you don't need to wait for is to be saved.

What you don't need to wait for is that golden nugget.

Instead, just know that you are worth it. You deserve the best life. You can have the best life. And I would like to help you.

You just have to say yes.

If you're ready then let's start.

First I want to tell you my story which is titled **'There's No Such Thing as the Right Time'**.

I've learnt that life is a constant balancing act. There is no such thing as achieving balance. It's just not possible as we cannot control everything. We only really have control over ourselves. Over what we think, what we say and how we behave.

At times in our life, the odd curveball will come our way. Our plans will not work out how we expected them to. People will not support us in the way we expected them to.

And that's why we need to be constantly balancing.

Remaining open and curious about what might happen rather than becoming rigid and risk becoming disillusioned and broken.

So, let me ask you, would you leave a successful career, working for a well-respected company, whilst on maternity leave with baby number two and without a plan?

That's exactly what I did in 2016. Brave or bonkers?

I'll let you decide because I know what I think.

It was all triggered by one of my earliest memories in my career, when I was driving to Uxbridge University to recruit some university students for internships at Rolls-Royce. I was accompanying a senior manager and, like most people, I wanted to know his story. It wasn't unusual. He'd started as an apprentice and gradually worked his way up through the ranks. Before he knew it, he'd gotten married, had children and was now at the age where the pension was too good for him to leave the company.

Oh my goodness. That's when it hit me. My immediate response was I am never going to be in a position like that where I felt like I had no choice and that I had no other options than to stay where I was. I decided there and then that I was not going to work for anyone for longer than five years. There was no way I was going to put myself in a position where I felt locked in.

Well fast-forward 17 years and I was in danger of turning into that person. You see, five years turned to 10 years, 10 years turned to 15 years and so on. During that time, I'd gotten married, I had a beautiful daughter and I was heavily pregnant with baby number two.

Don't get me wrong, I had a great career at Rolls-Royce. I worked on some really interesting projects including being part of the team that managed the build of the new production factory at Filton. Every time I pass the site, this is a great reminder of my career at Rolls-Royce.

One of the most challenging points in my career was when I project managed an engineering development programme. This really tested me. There was me, a non-engineer who knew very little about engineering, leading a group of intelligent and knowledgeable engineers to design, build, test and deliver a complex military aircraft engine. Now that's what you call a fish out of water. I remember having many sleepless nights. But at the end of the day, we delivered what was necessary to the customer and it felt amazing!

The last project that I worked on was one of my greatest achievements. I took this plain and uninspiring massive office space, that was occupied by over 200 individuals, and I led the team who turned it into a modern, versatile workspace that our colleagues would enjoy working in.

But the fact was, I still kept thinking about that moment in the car when I first started at Rolls-Royce. Now, more than ever, I thought I was in danger of being stuck in this company until retirement. And like the thousands of other times I'd remembered that initial conversation, I was questioning what I was doing. This wasn't the first time I was feeling like I was in the wrong career. This wasn't the first time I realised I wasn't supposed to be doing this. I knew something needed to change. But, unlike the other times, I was beginning to think the time *was* right. And, unlike other times I *did* feel brave enough to make that change.

However, it wasn't until I was about to go on maternity leave to have my baby boy, baby number two, that I really started thinking about where I was and where I wanted to go. Although maternity leave was imminent, I kept on thinking about what I was going to come back to afterwards. And I just couldn't face the thought of coming back. Coming back to this career.

You see, I sort of fell into working for Rolls-Royce. It wouldn't have necessarily been my first choice, but it was a good company with great benefits. I'd have job security. And it was just up the road from my family home, my parents were delighted. So it seemed like the obvious choice.

To be honest, I actually dreamed of working for a more forward-thinking company, like Virgin. One that provided a service or made a product that I knew more about, and one that I was passionate about. Aeroplane engines are impressive but it's not really my thing.

The more I thought about what I was coming back to after maternity leave, the more I thought I didn't want to come back. But what would I do if I didn't come back? Rolls-Royce was all I'd ever known. Well, other than working for my dad in our seaside restaurant.

It was too late; the seed was planted. Over the following months, all I could think about was what would be next?

Fortunately, whilst I was on maternity leave, the company was going through a redundancy programme. I saw this as the perfect opportunity to break free and to really go for what I wanted. Sort of.

What made this decision even more important was that although my children, Lea and Louka, at that point were very little, I wanted to be a good role model for them. I wanted them to go after their dreams. I wanted to encourage them to go after what they wanted. But how could I do that for them if I wasn't willing to do it for myself? So the decision was made, and with the support of my husband, I decided to take voluntary redundancy.

But I didn't really have a plan on what I was going to do next!

All I knew was I was going to take 2017 as a year to consciously decide what I wanted to do next. That was the only thing that I had planned. Crazy? Brave? At that point, all I knew was it felt right.

I know that not everyone is in a position to take a year out. But the choice to do something different is yours to make. How you start to make that change is up to you. You decide whether you hide away or make the most of life.

So 2017 was set to be my big adventure and to help me record my highs and lows, I decided to set up my Mummy on a Break Facebook page. I also wanted to use the opportunity to maybe inspire other mums to also be brave. Not to necessarily leave their jobs but be more aware of what their wants and needs were, other than being an amazing mum.

It was so liberating having a year off. A year to try different things out. To see what direction I wanted to go in.

I started volunteering for the Children's Hospital once a week for a couple of hours. I set up the Little Elves Festive Fair in support of CLIC

Sargent, which at the time of writing has raised nearly £4000.

One of the most important things I did was to work with a life coach, Anna.

Until I started working with Anna, I hadn't realised that I was wearing blinkers. I was not seeing all the opportunities that were available to me.

Anna questioned nearly all the assumptions that I'd been making about what I could and should do. She got me thinking about what was possible. And it's thanks to her that I even considered starting my journey as a business owner.

One of the first things she asked me was, 'What do you really want to do?' My answer: 'I wanted to start my own business.' But I didn't have an idea.

Wow. I didn't see that one coming.

Over the next few months, it became clear that I definitely wanted to start my own business. Why? I found myself looking at job ads and not feeling inspired whatsoever. Besides, retirement was still 25 years away. That's a long time and there was no way I was going to return to the same hamster wheel of the corporate world.

I also remember describing to Anna my retirement plan and saying, 'That's when I can do what I really want.' What? Wait 25 years to do what I really want? How ridiculous does that sound? Spend 25 years existing just to get to the point where I feel I can do what I really want.

Life is short. Twenty-five years could be a third of my life, what a waste.

That's what inspired me to throw caution to the wind and get on with things, like starting my first company, Fill That Space, although in 2020 I decided to close the company. That's what still inspires me today. Don't get me wrong, I'm not careless. I've got my eyes open. I'd never do anything to jeopardise the security of my family and my relationship. My husband is fully aware of what I want even if I can't always explain exactly what I'm doing.

I truly believe that if I hadn't met Anna and if I hadn't been brave enough to make my dreams a reality then I'd be in a very unhappy place. I'd be waking up every morning thinking 'here we go again.' Going to a job that paid the bills but left me feeling stifled and as if I was just a number.

Whereas today, things are so different. I love what I do. I love having the freedom that being a business owner gives me. And more importantly, I love being able to help.

I'm lucky. I was in a position where I could take that leap of faith. I could make changes immediately without really having a plan. Over the last few years, I've learnt so much and with the support of my family and friends, I'm now in a position where I actually feel like I'm living. I've taken back control – I'm now where I'm meant to be.

It's been emotional and I've had low moments. Moments where I just wanted to hide. But I've also had so many awesome moments. Moments that regularly remind me that leaving my job was the right decision.

Now I feel more comfortable in my skin. I feel better mentally and physically. And for me, it all comes down to mindset. The way I talk to myself, the way I view things and being open to what could be. Being aware of my actions and reactions so that I can be the best I can be, including being the best mum to my kids. Not perfect, just the best I can be.

I don't have to tell you that being a mum is not an easy job. There are times when I've questioned my decisions. When I've been annoyed at how I've behaved and responded to my children. When I've just not known what I should be doing.

However, being a mum is the best job in the world. I've laughed so hard that my insides have hurt. I've been given so many cuddles that I literally thought I'd burst. I've had the privilege of seeing the world differently and all because I listened.

Being a mum has given me one of the greatest opportunities to learn. Learn things about myself. Understand better what I think, say and do. Reflect on how I show up in life.

Although the list of things I've learnt is endless, I'm going to share the five I think have made a real difference to me and my family.

1. Being a busy mum and working hard isn't the answer.

Being busy, doing everything and working really, really hard means nothing if you're not present and living life. It's easy to fill time. But that's no fun.

My parents taught me that if you work hard then all will be okay because hard work always pays off. When I was younger, they had a busy seaside restaurant which meant working long hours and obviously working hard. All this effort paid off because they were very successful.

So that's been my work ethic. As children, we mirror what's around us. So as far as I was concerned being busy and working hard results in success! But I've learnt that it doesn't have to be this way. It's about focusing on what is important. Trying to do everything has literally exhausted me. It's made me question what I'm doing. At times, I've felt my only option was to withdraw, even give up.

What's stopped me is my children. Looking into my children's eyes and realising I'm missing out on life. They're growing up far too quickly and if I'm not careful I'll miss it.

So I choose to have peace in my life and focus on what is important and whenever I fall into being busy I stop, reflect and choose my next best move.

2. You're doing your best and that is more than good enough.

It's natural to compare ourselves with others so we can gauge whether we're doing a good job or not. The truth is, the most we can expect of ourselves is to do our best and that is enough.

I know I'm competitive. I want to do the best I can. I want to be the best and when it comes to being a mum, I definitely want to be the best. There's nothing like setting the bar high!

The truth is, doing the mummy juggle is hard as it is, without me piling on more pressure. I'm only human, I make mistakes and that's okay. I admit I've forgotten to pack my children's PE kit. I've got things wrong. But Lea and Louka are alive and smiling. That's what matters.

3. Your biggest challenge is you.

It's true, we can be our own worst enemy. The only person that ever really stands in your way is yourself. But you always have a choice even if you don't think so.

I've learnt and relearnt that I need to turn the volume down on my inner critic. The voice that is neither good nor bad. The voice that is just trying to keep me safe.

When I have listened to the voice, I've dwelled for too long in a negative space. I've wasted time feeling sorry for myself, instead of understanding what's going on and what my next best move is.

My inner voice will always be with me, especially as I attempt new things. However, I am free to choose how I respond.

4. Self-care is not a luxury.

There is always time for self-care because if you're running on empty you are no good to anyone.

I want to be a great role model for my kids. Which, for me, means leading by example. If I'm not looking after myself then what am I saying to them?

When my daughter was just a baby, I really wasn't looking after myself. At the end of the day, I would collapse on the sofa exhausted. I felt like I was constantly running on empty. But I had no idea how to change things. And to be honest, nothing really changed until my son came along!

I started to crave some of my old life back, before kids. That was the trigger to put me first and look after myself so I could be the best for them.

Self-care is not complicated and it doesn't have to be expensive. But you do need to make time.

5. Create healthy boundaries.

You don't have to be everything to everyone. You don't have to do everything. Focus on what is important and then create healthy boundaries to protect it.

I'm a bit of a people pleaser. I want everyone to be okay and if I can help make that happen then I'll do it. But it's not sustainable. And it also means that you're sacrificing yourself for others. You're demoting yourself for others. That's really not okay. The most important person in your life will always be you.

I was working long hours; I was getting involved with everything and I was trying to do everything. The only way life was going to be different was to do things differently. Which was to create healthy boundaries, deciding what was okay and what was not.

The truth is, life is one long learning journey. We try stuff out. We experience things. We take what works, we change things and hopefully, we throw the rest away. Life is not meant to be perfect. Life is full of challenges, of ups and downs, of twists and turns.

Life is meant to be interesting. It is for living and about fully embracing whatever comes your way and making the best of it with what you know.

So, what have you learnt and how would you describe your life right now?

Amazing, awesome, calm, peaceful, exciting.

Or

Boring, dull, uninspiring, mundane, hard work.

Or

Alright, okay, fine, not bad, nice.

How does that make you feel?

Before I went on maternity leave with baby number two, my word would have been alright. Or maybe fine. Or even okay. And I thought that was good.

As long as I had enough and everyone seemed happy then I thought that was good enough!

And there it is. Good enough.

Having spent some time, post having baby number two, deciding what I really wanted from life, I realised that okay was not good enough. I wanted more. I deserved more and I knew I could have more.

And as you know that triggered a change in direction and the next leg of my journey through life.

For some reason, most of us settle for okay. Maybe it's because we don't think we deserve more or maybe it's because we don't want to be greedy. Maybe it's because we don't want to stand out by being different.

Whatever the excuse, I'm here to tell you that you deserve great and I can help you get it.

Let's look at it a different way.

When you were a child, what did you want to be?

Now you're an adult, what are you?

Growing up, I wanted to be a music teacher. Then a solicitor. And then one night, having had a dream where I was wearing a suit standing outside a tall skyscraper, I decided to go into business!

At the time, my interpretation of my dream led me to study business studies at university. Mainly because I really didn't know what I wanted to be so studying a general subject would surely open many doors and I could try different things.

Well, it opened one door and I was there for 17 years. Thinking all was good.

The truth is, I'd become comfortable. Life was okay. I didn't really have any worries.

The truth is, I would wake up most mornings thinking, is this it?

The truth is, I didn't have a reason to change.

Well, not until I had baby number two and I realised that if I was going to be a great role model to Lea and Louka I needed to do something.

Life now is definitely different. I feel uncomfortable a lot of the time but I'm enjoying the ride. And that's what counts.

You see it's easy to accept the hand we're dealt and continue going through the motions. However, what does that lead to?

Autopilot.

Feeling numb.

Sleepwalking through life.

Wouldn't it be great to be living a life full of love, laughter and adventure? Where every day is full of excitement? Where every day feels like you are living your dreams?

Surely the answer must be yes.

But how to start?

You know the hardest part is starting. But once you've taken that first step you'll be in motion, you'll find your momentum and then it'll become easier.

Find the imbalance

You now know that life is a balancing act and so there will be areas of imbalance in your life that you'll naturally want to rebalance. Decide which area this is. What's important to you? What's your priority? Where are you lacking energy?

Decide what you want

Once you know your starting point, it's then about deciding where you want to go. Use all your senses to decide what your destination looks like and feels like. See it in colour. Hear it. Fully immerse yourself in the feeling of where you are trying to go.

Take small steps

Now to take that first step. Decide on an easy first step that will help you make that change. Something you know you can achieve. Then keep on taking steps and make them slightly more challenging each time.

Stay focused but flexible

Like water, we need to remain focused but able to bend and turn in line with the curveballs of life. Know that your journey will not be a straight path and expect life to challenge you on the way.

Celebrate the change

Life is about having fun, which means it's more important to enjoy the journey than reach the destination. Wake up every day with an open mind, ready to take part in the adventures and celebrate whatever the day has to offer.

Changing your life doesn't have to be difficult. You don't have to wait for a life altering event before you decide you deserve better. There is nothing wrong with wanting more.

I know that I'm not alone in how I felt. You see, as mums, we're very good at putting the needs of everyone else ahead of our own. It's what we do. It's in our DNA. After all, back in the day when the men were out hunting, the women were looking after things. It's our default position.

That's why I now help other mums who are feeling the same. Mums who are stuck. Mums who want to make changes. Mums who just need that helping hand to take action. You see, sometimes you know something is missing but you don't know what it is. I help busy working mums find out what it is and then help them to take action, so that they can do something about it.

And that is what this book is all about.

This book will take you on a journey to discover where the imbalance is in your life and help you determine how you can correct it, so you can have the life you want. I want to help you easily navigate to a life where you wake up every morning excited by what the day may have in store. Instead of just climbing back onto the treadmill of life and going through the motions.

This book is split into three sections:

Part 1: Feel free to dream

This is about guiding you through a process of understanding where you are today and where you'd like to be when it comes to Work, Relationships, Money Matters, Wellness and the Fun Stuff. By the end of this section, you will clearly know what you want to move away from and what you are trying to move toward.

Part 2: Making your dream a reality

Now we start to get into the detail. This part will take each aspect from above and get you thinking more deeply about what it is you really want. You will need to use all your senses to really feel, see, hear, smell and even taste what you're trying to achieve. This is where you get to decide what actions you will take to move you closer to your dreams becoming a reality.

Part 3: Crushing the challenges that will get in your way

And finally, during your journey there will be moments where you come up against challenges, brick walls and blocks. This part of the book will help you to overcome those times. Whether you notice symptoms of comparisonitis, or that your inner voice is too loud. I have lots of tips for you on how you can manage those times.

And finally, throughout this book I have included pages for you to write on. Use these pages to capture your thoughts as well as answering the questions I ask at the end of each section and the guided exercises in part 1 and part 2.

It's now time to create and live the life you deserve.

FEEL FREE TO DREAM

"If you obey all the rules, you'll miss all the fun."

Katharine Hepburn

Before you can start on this journey, to change your life as you know it, I want you to be able to shake off some of the baggage that you are carrying. The stuff that you have picked up along the way.

I want you to realise that you are more than the roles you play in your life. I want you to be able to reacquaint yourself with who you really are and remember the things you enjoyed doing.

I want you to accept that it's okay to put yourself first. You too deserve to have your wants and needs met, without putting your life on hold whilst you support those who you love.

I want you to remember what's important to you. What really matters to you. Who really matters to you. Where you actually want to focus your energy.

I want you to be able to believe in yourself. To get what you want so that you know that you deserve to have whatever you want. It's not selfish and it's not greedy.

I want you to be comfortable with being the lead actor in your life. There is no need to be the observer. Only you can be the lead actor, which doesn't mean being loud. It means having the courage to decide what's next that suits you.

And finally, I want you to embrace your ability to dream. To see in colour what you want to happen before it happens in reality. Because if you know where you're going it will be so much easier to get there.

You see, anything is possible if you really want it. Your dreams can come true. You have the power to create the life you want.

It's waiting. Are you ready?

Let's demolish the barriers that stand in your way and build the life that you thought was only real in your dreams.

YOU ARE MORE THAN
JUST A MUMMY

"Being a mama can be tough, but always remember in the eyes of your child, no one does it better than you."

Unknown

Are you a mum, a wife, a sister, a friend, a business owner, an employee, a housekeeper, a cook, an organiser, a neighbour, a taxi driver?

Being a mum, you're probably most of these, if not all of them.

Are you trying to be everything to everyone?

You must be tired.

Taking on all these roles is not only exhausting but it helps you avoid doing what is most important.

Being you.

But that's okay because you don't have the time anyway. You're probably so busy with everyone else that you've left no time for yourself!

Why is it?

Is that okay?

What would happen if you did something different?

What if you stopped trying to be everything to everyone?

Now, I love being a mum. For a long time, I saw it as my main role. My only role! And I'm lucky because I'm blessed to have awesome children who love me unconditionally and who ground and challenge me daily. I love spending time with them and giving them everything they need. However, I can only do that because I also do the same for myself.

You see, I am first an individual. I am first Maria. And I know that I need to be the best for myself before I can be the best for anyone else. Then I can give my best to everyone I love.

Simple, yet this is not something that mums typically do.

As mums, we can choose to live in the shadow of mum guilt. Thinking we're being selfish if we put ourselves first. Thinking we're not good enough. Thinking we're not doing our best. But it doesn't have to be this way.

I would like you to give yourself permission to step out of the shadows and know it is okay to be you. Because you are good enough, you always do your best and because putting yourself first is necessary.

You see, when we start our mum journey, we feel like we have no choice but to put our children before us. We worry about being judged, about doing the right thing and about being compared.

The truth is, none of that matters. We are all on our own journey and being a mum doesn't mean you have to lose yourself, who you are and what you want.

How would it feel if you took some simple steps to reacquaint yourself with you? To remember who you are and what you like.

Here are some suggestions you can try to get you started.

Have me-time

Make sure you have some me-time as part of your day, no matter how challenging this may feel. Even if it's just a 5 minute walk or 5 minutes alone in the bathroom! You need time for yourself, even if it's just to be able to think and reflect without being interrupted.

Take care of yourself

It's all about self-care, which doesn't have to be expensive or fancy. It's about embracing the simple things in life that help you to fill your cup, allow you to protect and improve your wellbeing and remind you to also care for yourself.

> You can download my free guide, 'Why self-care is not selfish! 30 feel good for FREE habits' from my website
> www.mummyonabreak.co.uk

Make a list

Write down all the things you love about yourself, even if it's the shape of your eyebrows. Not only are you good enough but you are great. Sometimes you just need to remind yourself.

Daydream

Daydreaming is amazing. It makes us feel good. It allows us to create without boundaries, restrictions or limitations. Dream about all the things you love. Dream about all the things you want and all the things you want to do.

You are not defined by the roles that you play. You are definitely more than 'just' a mummy. You are an individual who deserves to be living the life you want.

If you're ready to do that then next you need to get comfortable putting yourself first. I know, scary. But you can do it. Only you can give yourself permission. It's not only right for you, but also right for those who you care about and who genuinely want you to be happy.

LEARNING TO BREATHE

"Breathe. Let go. And remind yourself that this very moment is the only one you know you have for sure."

Oprah Winfrey

Let me ask you a question, what would happen if you couldn't breathe?

Would it force you to stop?

Would you persevere until you had no choice?

Would you ask why?

Let's look at it in a different way. During the air steward's flight safety demonstration, they always say put your oxygen mask on first before attempting to help anyone else.

It's simple. If you can't breathe then how can you help anyone else?

They don't say, help everyone else first whilst you struggle to breathe!

And that's true in life too. If you're not looking after yourself then eventually you won't be able to look after those you love. And not only that, what example are you setting for others? For the wonderful people in your life who see you as their role model and who you want the best for.

So it's ironic, that when we become a mummy we immediately put ourselves at the bottom of this virtual list. We insist on making sure that everyone else's needs are satisfied first and then wonder why we're too tired or lack time to do anything about our own needs.

I love to help. I've always loved to help. Helping others makes me happy. And if there's a problem, I'm there lending a hand and trying to figure out what the solution is. I'm ready and willing to put my needs aside to make sure that everyone else is okay.

This is a lovely quality to have, but only if we're also helping ourselves and making sure that our needs are being met as well. To make sure that we're also okay. To make sure that we're getting the help that we need. Remember, if we're not looking after ourselves then how can we expect to be able to help others?

The thing is, our needs are just as important as those we love, yet we'd never dream of not supporting them. So why do it to ourselves?

Is it that you think you're not important?

Is it that you don't think you're worth it?

Is it that you think you can wait?

Whatever your reason, I can tell you it's just an excuse. An excuse that is making it okay to put yourself at the bottom of the list. No one is forcing you to be at the bottom of the list.

Only you can decide where you are on this list, so stop putting yourself at the bottom.

But where to start?

I want to keep it really simple at this point so that you can start to create good habits that will support you in life.

Create good boundaries

It's important to have simple and clear boundaries. Boundaries that stop us from saying no to ourselves and yes to everybody else. Boundaries that clearly protect us and help us to meet our needs.

It could be as simple as finishing work at a set time every day. It could be as simple as going for an uninterrupted daily walk. It could be as simple as going to bed at 10pm every night.

Bookend the day like a hug

It's all about starting and ending your day in the best possible way. Starting the day in such a way that you are ready to handle whatever the day might bring. Ending the day calmly so that you can have a restful night's sleep.

We all know that you can't drink from an empty cup, and when it comes to our well-being we need to be practising habits that allow us to fill our cup. That's why having easy morning and nighttime daily routines can help us to feel energised and calm.

This could be stretching first thing in the morning to physically wake your body before you do anything else. It might be saying daily affirmations to focus your mind and set your intentions for the day. Or it could be journaling before bed to let go of the day's stresses.

Invest in you

You wouldn't think twice about showing others that you think they're worth it. However, how often do you show yourself that you're worth it? You may see it as treating yourself but in fact you're investing in yourself.

Whether this is investing in your mind, body or soul, it's important and it doesn't have to mean spending any money either. It might just be about giving yourself some space and time each day for just you.

Embrace your tribe

It's so important to surround yourself with the right people. The type of people who will lift you up and who have your back. That's not a crowd of 'yes' people, but people who will be honest and who genuinely want what's best for you.

They're the ones that help you fill your cup, that make you smile and make your heart sing.

Listen to your body

Our bodies are amazing and communicate with us regularly. They have the power to heal and put us back into balance when we get a knock. So if you notice a niggle, don't assume it will go away. Stop and take the time to understand what is going on. Because doing something when the body whispers is easier than when it starts shouting.

As you can see, there are many simple things you can do to help yourself. This is your first step to taking action, to ensure that you sometimes feature in the top spot. Because if you don't put yourself there no one else will.

So tell me, what is the first thing you will do for yourself today?

Once you have accepted that you too deserve to be first, you then need to decide what really matters to you and what you think is important.

What is the first thing you will do for yourself today?

_____

_____

_____

_____

_____

_____

_____

_____

_____

_____

_____

_____

_____

_____

_____

_____

_____

_____

_____

_____

FIGURING OUT WHAT'S REALLY IMPORTANT

"The most important thing is to enjoy your life - to be happy - it's all that matters."

Audrey Hepburn

When was the last time you stopped to think and asked yourself, what really matters to you?

When I first became a mum, my world revolved around my daughter. I'd been given this beautiful gift which I promised I would nurture, protect and love.

I was aware of her every breath. I wanted to fulfil her every need. I wanted to make sure she was always safe. After all, I'd become a mum, she was my responsibility and this was my duty.

The problem was, with time, I'd forgotten about myself and I hadn't even realised it. I was a busy working mum. I had no time! Now, you may think, but that's okay. You're a mum. Your children are supposed to be your number one.

Well, that's what I thought. I now think differently.

31

The thing is, the most important person in your life is you.

This is true for everyone, no matter who you are. After all, it's your life. You are the lead actor, no one else. The stage is yours. Only you can decide how the story plays out.

If nothing else, just remember you are a role model to your children. If you don't think you are important enough in your life, what are you telling them?

But what about the judgement from others?

It's not about what other people think. It's not about what other people say. It's not about what other people do.

It's really easy to get sucked into what is going on outside when what matters is what's going on inside us.

What we think.

What we do.

What we say.

That's what matters.

It matters if you are happy with yourself. If you are speaking to yourself with compassion and you are able to speak to others from a place of kindness. If you're doing what makes you happy and you're living in the now, then you'll know that anything is possible.

I know life can seem hectic and it's easy to become disconnected from who we are and what we want. We get swept along with life and forget to stop and acknowledge what we have, what we want and where we're going next.

You have come a long way and you don't know it. You are a different person from who you were 10, 20 and 30 years ago. You have changed over time. You have evolved.

And what has happened during that time? What have you experienced? What have you achieved?

If you took the time to really understand who you are now and stay focused on all the positives, you'd realise that you're already an amazing woman. An amazing woman with lots of gifts that need to be shared with the world.

Taking time out to not only appreciate who you are, but also what you want is not just necessary, it's vital. Why intentionally choose to amble through life when you could take the bull by the horns and make life happen? Be the one in the driver's seat deciding where you're going and which turns are best for you.

I know this is a big question so start small. Start with what feels easy.

Wouldn't that be better than just going with it? That's what happens when you become stuck on the treadmill of life. You just need to find the emergency stop button and have the courage to press it.

Life is for living and to do that we need to be conscious of who we are and what is going on. We need to be conscious of where we want to go.

However, it's not always easy to stop. And when you do, then what's the next step?

My advice is simple: if you think you're important, you will find the time. Here are some suggestions to get you started.

Gratitude

Write a list of ten things you are grateful for. This will show you what is important to you. This will remind you of what is important to you. Then it's up to you to ensure you have more of it in your life.

You have plenty in life to be grateful for. Start with the simple things and start with you. You come first, remember. If it helps, look in the mirror and look yourself in the eye. The woman staring back at you deserves your full attention. Tell her why she is great.

Then you can focus on the wonderful people who are in your life. The experiences you have had. The fact that you get to wake up every day and have the choice to decide what's next.

Values

Understand what your values are. Knowing your values helps you to make decisions and take actions that are right for you. When we decide or take action that is in alignment with our values, then life flows in the right way for us. Life becomes easy.

You can recall times in your life when your decisions or actions just didn't feel right or sit well with you. That's probably because they were against your values. Being more aware of your values will minimise and even remove those awkward feelings and situations.

Passions

Write a list of what you're passionate about. What you love doing. Then make time for them in your life. Doing what you love will always make you feel good. It will keep you grounded and in the here and now. You will always have the time and energy for the things that make your heart sing and put a smile on your face. And guess what? This will also benefit your loved ones. They will want to share in what you have and be part of your joy.

Send a letter

Write a letter from your future self describing the wonderful life you are living. This is such a powerful exercise that will open your eyes to how you really want life to be, instead of what you think life should be like. The key here is to let the pen do the work, without limitations or restrictions.

To make more of this, imagine how you would feel receiving this letter. How amazing it would be to know that the words in the letter were describing the life you have had.

Wishes

And finally, write a list of three wishes that you'd like to make come true. You are your own Fairy Godmother. You have the power to make your wishes a reality. So instead of just wishing, go make them happen by taking the first step.

Make that first step easy. Remember, you're more likely to be successful and achieve what you want if you make it easy. Then you can just keep taking small steps until all three of your wishes have come true.

Life is what you make it. If you know what matters, then creating the life you want and living it is so much easier.

So tell me, what really matters to you?

It's great when you actually realise what matters and what's important. However, you may be feeling a little stuck on how to make that change and committing to making it happen. And that's what's next.

What really matters to you?

_____

_____

_____

_____

_____

_____

_____

_____

_____

_____

_____

_____

_____

_____

_____

_____

_____

_____

_____

_____

_____

_____

_____

_____

_____

HOW TO GET WHAT
YOU WANT

"Nothing makes you realize you don't know what you want more than getting what you want."

Jane Wagner

Do you wake up every morning feeling grateful for what you have?

Do you wake up every morning appreciating how far you've come?

Do you wake up every morning knowing that you have what you deserve?

I hope you answered yes. But what if it was no?

Is it because you don't have anything to be grateful for?

Is it because you feel like you've gone backwards in life not forwards?

Is it because you know you deserve more?

The truth is, life is based on the decisions we make, the choices we make and on what we do next.

If you want to turn the 'no' into a 'yes' and you want things to be different, then start making different choices. Where you go next is completely up to you.

Let me ask you some different questions.

Do you ever reflect on life?

On where you want to go?

On how far you've come?

On what you have right now?

You may have said all the time, occasionally, or never.

Giving ourselves some time and space to reflect is so important. It helps us to be grateful for what we have and what we have achieved and to feel good about ourselves. It helps us to get ourselves back on track whenever we feel like we've lost our way.

And finally, have you ever thought:

How did I get here?

Where am I going?

I'm never going to get to where I want to go!

These thoughts are part of what I like to call 'the observer's life'. An individual who is being swept along by life, who is letting others determine their course and who is stuck on the treadmill.

But it doesn't have to be this way. This is your life and you have the power to determine where you are going and how you get there.

So let me make it easy for you.

Visualise

Before you do anything, you need to decide what you want your life to look like. This is your opportunity to dream. To consider what life will hold for you. What you really want. No restrictions. No limitations. No constraints.

Give yourself permission to have fun and see where it leads you.

Choose one thing

Your dream life will have lots of wonderful things in it. However, you can only really change one thing at a time. It is much easier to focus on one thing at one time and you will see more progress than if you try doing lots of things at the same time.

So what is the one thing you want to change right now? What is the one thing that will motivate you to make a change? The one thing you know you can change from now?

Take the first step

If you want to actually make a change, you need to have a plan that will guide you to make that change.

I love a plan. It makes my life easier. It actually gives me freedom. It means I don't have to think. So what does your plan look like for a making change?

A plan is great, but can be meaningless until you take action. It's all about taking that first step, which is the hardest part. That first step gets you one step closer to your dream. It also doesn't matter what size that first step is. It definitely doesn't have to be a grand gesture. The important thing is that you took the first step. The rest will then seem a lot easier.

Your tribe

Making a change can be hard but is easier when you're surrounded by people who want you to succeed. Share what you are doing with those you trust so that they can cheer you on, no matter what your progress is. It's all about making your life easier.

So you see, where you are today doesn't have to be where you are tomorrow. You have the power to change things. It's up to you.

What will make you start to make your dreams a reality?

You may still be feeling like you haven't got the courage to step into the light. To take that first step forward. Well, I'm here to tell you that you have the courage and you can do it. It's time to stop being the spectator in your life and take on the leading role.

What three things do you most want from life?

_____

_____

_____

_____

_____

_____

_____

_____

_____

_____

_____

_____

_____

_____

_____

_____

_____

_____

_____

_____

_____

_____

HAPPY TO BE A
⇘ SPECTATOR ⇙

"Life gives us choices. You either grab on with both hands and just go for it, or you sit on the sidelines."

Christine Feehan

I believe that everyone should be the star of their life. After all, it is your life and so you should be up front and centre stage. However, so many of us insist on sitting in the audience watching what is going on rather than grabbing life with both hands and making it what we want it to be.

So why do you insist on sitting in the audience?

Is it that you're more comfortable being in the audience?

Does it feel safe?

Do you think that's where you should be?

Have you decided it's too late to do anything else?

Whatever it may be, the truth is the stage is yours and waiting for you. The truth is, the only person that can get you on the stage, in your life, is you.

Let me just be clear here, this doesn't literally mean being the centre of attention shouting, 'Look at me! Look at me!' It's got nothing to do with being an extrovert or a showoff. It means being more decisive and purposeful in your life. Going with the flow is great, but what if it's not in the direction you want to go?

So the question is, what are you really waiting for?

When it comes to your life, it is really all about you. So why have you given that responsibility to someone else? Because by sitting in the audience, that's what you're doing. And more importantly, why would you not want to be the one who determines what happens in your life?

Let's look at it in a different way.

If you were to fast forward your life to when you're taking your last breath, what do you want to remember?

Is it a life full of laughs and dreams fulfilled? Or is it one full of regrets? You decide.

Yes, the choice is yours.

You get to take action now so that your life is what you want it to be.

Surely it is better to regret something that you've done as opposed to something you haven't.

For me, it's very simple, the lead role is yours. No need to audition. However, it's your choice whether you commit to being the star or simply watching life happen. Accepting whatever life throws at you, allowing yourself to just get swept along and accepting that 'what will be, will be'.

I invite you to ask yourself, is this what you really want? Are you happy with how things are? Are you happy, making sure others are happy without wanting the same for yourself?

If your answer is no, then I would like to help. I want you to have the confidence to be the star of the show and determine what your life looks like now instead of, say, waiting until the kids have left home.

It's about taking small steps so you can get started.

Understand why you're in the audience

There will be a reason why you are happier sitting in the audience. So the first challenge is to know why. You can do this by asking yourself why, over and over again, until you find out the real why.

I highly recommend writing this down or journaling. You could even use journal prompts to help. For example, why do I let others take the lead? What is stopping me from going after what I want? What would happen if I just went for it?

How can you change this?

Then the real work starts. Deciding what you're going to do to change. Whether this is to undo some deep-rooted beliefs or change habits that are not serving you.

Maybe you've identified a common theme that seems to be holding you back. If so, this is where your focus needs to be.

What would it take?

The next step is to get you onto the stage. What would it take to get you there? What actions do you need to take to get you moving? Is it as simple as figuring out what you want?

Who can help?

It's not always easy to get started, so enlist the help of people you trust to guide you and hold you accountable. Although I encourage my clients to develop an inner cheerleader, having others to also be your cheerleader makes it a lot easier when you're starting.

When will you start?

I've said it before, starting is the hardest part and by taking small steps anything is possible. So make a commitment to yourself by starting today and promise that you will not give up. When you fall over, you will get up, learn and then keep going. When something positive happens you will celebrate and bottle that feeling forever.

Whether you believe you only have one life or have many, it's yours and it is up to you to make it what you want it to be. That is your responsibility.

Are you ready to take on the starring role?

Now that you know only you can be the star in your story, I want you to let go and leave behind anything that is holding you back. I want you to accept that anything is possible. I want you to commit to dreaming big.

Are you ready to take on the starring role?

ARE YOU READY
TO DREAM?

"A year from now you may wish you had started today."

Karen Lamb

By now, you will have realised that all I want from you and for you is to make the decision to put yourself first occasionally and go do the thing that you want to do. I've gently guided you through what might be holding you back, what may make you feel uncertain and what might be stopping you.

Now is your time to be brave, to find the courage that is already within you and say yes to what you want from life.

We are the authors of our own story. The directors of our film. The conductors of our life's soundtrack. This means that we have the ability to create the life we want, even if it doesn't always feel like it. It is up to us to define what we want and then go make it happen.

The responsibility of what happens next rests firmly in your hands. No one is going to wave a magic wand and make it happen for you.

I want to be honest with you, change isn't easy. The status quo is easy. The brain will naturally take the path of least resistance. This means more often than not our brain will guide us to take the easy option, which isn't always the right option for us.

The easy option will mean less effort, it will also mean staying where you are. It's accepting that if you always do what you've always done then you'll always get what you've always got. It's like banging your head against a brick wall and expecting something other than a headache!

Hopefully, by now you will have realised that I am about being compassionate as well as giving some tough love. The reason for that is I know that change is hard, especially as your actions will have an impact on others. But if you're going to get to where you want to go then you need someone who will hold you accountable and tell you the truth.

As I say to my clients, if you want to get something off your chest go and speak to your mum, sister, auntie, grandma, cousin or friend. However, if you want to make a shift then come to me.

I will hold your hand and guide you to where you want to go. I will be the first one to celebrate your success. I will also be the first one to tell you if something doesn't seem to be working.

If you really want what you're about to design, then you need to commit to it 100 per cent. That's the only way that you'll get what you want. If you just dip your toe in, it's the same as doing nothing. The decision really is yours.

It's time to take that first step.

To begin with, I first want you to acknowledge where you are in life right now. See what is good and what needs attention. Find the imbalance in your life. What do you think is your priority and will take your focus first? That way you then have something to compare with as you progress on your journey.

I want you to think about the following five areas of your life: Work, Relationships, Wellness, Money Matters and the Fun Stuff.

Work

What 'work' is has evolved so much since I got my first job. No longer is it necessarily a 9 to 5 job working for someone else. It means different things to different people. Today we have many options. It's just figuring out what we want and need and how we can make it a reality. It's about not thinking conventionally but maybe being a bit creative. Whether you're an employee, employer, business owner, full-time mum / housewife or carer.

Are you where you want to be right now?

Wellness

It's far too easy to look after everyone else and forget about yourself. The problem is that you're no good to anyone if you're exhausted and generally running on low energy. It's important to look after your mental health and physical health.

This doesn't mean adding more things to your daily routine. It means working out what is right for you and what you enjoy doing so that your wellness is a priority.

How are you taking care of yourself?

Money Matters

Life is not free. But it's amazing what you can achieve if you are in control of your money. You're able to make better decisions, your options are more visible and you know what is possible. You can have peace of mind.

Whether you are a saver or a spender, knowing your finances will make life less stressful.

What is your relationship like with your money?

Relationships

We have so many individuals in our lives. Some are very important, some are hard work and some are with us regardless of how we feel. The key is understanding who they are and how we want our relationships to be, so that we can then manage them. This may sound mechanical but it's surprising how much easier relationships are when our eyes are open and we know what we're doing.

Who are you spending time with?

The Fun Stuff

It's time to nourish the real you. To focus on your happiness. What makes you laugh? What do you enjoy doing? What puts a spring in your step? What would you do if you didn't feel so tired or if you had time?

As I've said before, life is about the journey and enjoying it.

Where is the fun in your life?

You should now be thinking about the different areas of your life, what they mean to you and maybe even what you'd like them to be like.

You probably already have an idea as to where the imbalance is and which aspect you would like to focus on next. Let me help you affirm that.

What one thing do you want from your work, wellness, money matters, relationships and the fun stuff?

_____

_____

_____

_____

_____

_____

_____

_____

_____

_____

_____

_____

_____

_____

_____

_____

_____

_____

_____

_____

_____

_____

_____

_____

A DESIGN FOR LIFE

"Lead a life of your own design, on your own terms.
Not one that others or the environment have scripted
for you."

Tony Robbins

The words of Eckhart Tolle regularly ground me. He said, 'The only thing you ever have is now.' Yesterday has already happened and cannot be changed. The future is yet to happen and rests on what you do right now. Which just goes to show how important now is.

If you're dwelling on the past, then you are stopping yourself from moving forward. And if you're living in the future then you are missing the opportunities that are right in front of you.

Before you can design the life you want, we need to start by acknowledging the now. Where are you right now when it comes to all aspects of your life? Your Work, Wellness, Relationships, Money Matters and the Fun Stuff?

Where is the imbalance?

How do you feel?

Are you starting on solid ground or is it a bit shaky?

As you know, I assumed my imbalance was my work. Although I'd had a great career, I always felt like a square peg in a round hole. I'd been given the opportunity to work in this amazing company with a prestigious reputation, so I just got on with it. I worked hard and my efforts were rewarded.

But I always had that feeling that something wasn't quite right. At times, I felt like a foreigner. I felt like they were speaking a different language to me. So to start with, my focus was on my work. What did I want it to look like? What work did I want to be doing? Who did I want to be working for?

You may or may not know where the imbalance is in your life right now. Either way it doesn't matter, because I'm going to guide you through a life assessment. This will either confirm what you already know or allow you to identify what is more important for you.

Whilst doing this exercise, I ask just one thing of you: remain open-minded and curious as I guide you through reviewing all aspects of your life using my Wheel of Life.

The Wheel of Life is an assessment tool that focuses on the five aspects that I think make up your life, which I have already mentioned. They are Work, Wellness, Money Matters, Relationships and the Fun Stuff.

If you're ready, it's now time for you to complete your assessment and see where the imbalance might be in your life.

Wheel of Life Assessment

You may already be familiar with completing a life assessment. It certainly isn't uncommon. Below you will see the Wheel of Life that I have created.

The difference with the way I do it is, you will complete the assessment twice. For the first assessment, you will need to answer the five specific questions against each of the five aspects, which will give you a total against each aspect. The main reason for this is so you can see whether you have a good foundation in place.

Asking these specific questions, where you can only answer yes or no, also aims to take the emotion out of the assessment. It is important to do it this way because how you're feeling when you complete the assessment can influence how you respond and may not give you a true assessment.

However, it is also important that you acknowledge how life feels right now. That's why you need to do a second assessment. The second time you will complete the assessment by deciding on a scale of 0-10 how happy you are against each aspect. You see, although you might be doing all the 'right things', they may not be right for you. You might just be going through the motions because someone said that's what you should be doing.

Next, you will plot the outcome of both assessments on one chart which will then show you where the imbalance is in your life. I suggest you use a different colour for each assessment so that you can tell them easily apart. Seeing both assessments on one diagram will make it easier for you to prioritise what you could focus on first.

Completing this assessment will give you insight into what's really going on, how you feel and what might be stopping you from moving forward.

So, grab a pen or pencil, find a quiet space, make yourself comfortable and let's begin.

Assessment One

Below are the steps you need to follow to complete the first assessment. It is important that you read all of the steps before you start.

- Step 1: Answer all the questions - read each question carefully and answer either yes or no. Give yourself two points for each question where you answered yes. Make sure you are completely honest and remember it's either yes or no. No sitting on the fence.

- Step 2: Calculate your score - add up the scores in each section to give you five totals, each one is out of 10.
- Step 3: Record your scores on the wheel - mark a cross on the central line of the Wheel of Life below against each aspect then join up all the crosses.

As you complete the assessment, use the lined pages at the end of this section to note the following:

- Notice any positive or negative thoughts you had.
- List any assumptions you may be making.
- Record any aspirations you may have.

Wheel of Life Questions

Work   Yes / No

1. Does your work support your life priorities?
2. Does your work meet your work needs?
3. Does your work give you tangible and non-tangible benefits?
4. Are you working in the field you want?
5. Are you earning your desired salary?

Total:

Relationships   Yes / No

1. Do you have mostly good relationships?
2. Do you enjoy spending time with the individuals in your life?
3. Are you energised by your relationships?
4. Are you yourself when spending time with others?
5. Do you focus your attention on those who are your supporters?

Total:

Money Matters   Yes / No

1. Do you know what your monthly income and expenditure is?
2. Have you set yourself a monthly budget?
3. Do you try to get the most from your money?
4. Do you regularly have a surplus at the end of each month?
5. Are you regularly saving money and investing it?

Total:

Wellness   Yes / No

1. Do you have a morning wake up routine?
2. Do you drink plenty of water?
3. Are you physically active during the week?
4. Do you eat a varied diet?

5. Do you have an evening wind down routine?

Total:

The Fun Stuff   Yes / No

1. Do you find you have spare time for yourself
    outside your work and other commitments?
2. Are you able to fill your spare time?
3. Do you have hobbies and interests you enjoy?
4. Do you regularly do things that make you laugh
    and put a smile on your face?
5. Do you find that you always have the time and
    energy to do the things that you enjoy?

Total:

Wheel of Life

Use these pages to note the following having completed the life assessment:

- Notice any positive or negative thoughts you had.
- List any assumptions you may be making.
- Record any aspirations you may have.

_____

_____

_____

_____

_____

_____

_____

_____

_____

_____

_____

_____

_____

_____

_____

_____

_____

_____

_____

_____

_____

_____

Assessment Two

Below are the steps you need to follow to complete the second assessment. It is important that you read all of the steps before you start the assessment.

- Step 1: Score each aspect - decide on a scale of 0-10 how happy you are in that aspect, with 0 being completely unhappy and 10 being ecstatic.
- Step 2: Record your scores on the wheel - mark a cross on the central line on the same Wheel of Life against each aspect then join up all the crosses, but this time use a different colour pen or pencil.

As before, when you're completing the assessment, use the lined pages at the end of this section to note the following:

- Notice any positive or negative thoughts you had.
- Be aware of assumptions you may be making.
- Acknowledge any aspirations you may have.

Wheel of Life Happiness Assessment

Happiness	Score 0-10
Work	
Relationships	
Money Matters	
Wellness	
The Fun Stuff	

Use these pages to note the following having completed the life assessment:

- Notice any positive or negative thoughts you had.
- List any assumptions you may be making.
- Record any aspirations you may have.

_____

_____

_____

_____

_____

_____

_____

_____

_____

_____

_____

_____

_____

_____

_____

_____

_____

_____

_____

_____

_____

_____

_____

You can now see both assessments on one page, so let's delve a little deeper.

Using the lined paper on the following pages, I would like you to answer these questions.

1. How do you feel about what you see?
2. Does this feel / seem right and why is that?
3. Does what you see surprise you?
4. Does this give you insight into how you are feeling about your life?
5. Which area would you say is your priority when it comes to making a change?

Life Assessment Comparison

You now know a lot more about where you are today and probably what is holding you back.

I invite you to change things. This is your opportunity to let go of anything that might be holding you back from having what you want. The shoulds, woulds and coulds. This is your time to dig deep and allow yourself to dream. To put pen to paper and determine what you want life to be like, in full colour and with the volume turned up.

I would like you to read the passage below and as you're doing that, I would like you to really visualise what the words mean to you. Use all your senses to make what you are reading real. Feel the emotions that come up for you. See the colours and movement of what you are reading. Hear the voices of the people that may come up.

My Desired Life

'I have a career that I have always dreamed of. I have found my purpose and am grateful that I get to choose what I do every day. I go to work every day knowing that I'm doing what I was meant to do. And as a bonus, I'm getting paid what I'm worth. This gives me freedom and flexibility to pick and choose what I do, when I do it and with who.

I am also now more comfortable with my money as it flows freely into my life. I've become skilled in managing my money. I am easily able to make it grow, and it can feel like I do actually have a money tree in my garden. I have developed a really healthy relationship with money. I am able to do things that I never dreamed of, as well as invest in others and share my wealth with others.

My life now is fruitful in so many ways, but especially because of the relationships that I have and treasure in my life. I am surrounded by wonderful, loving people who lift me up and enjoy sharing and celebrating in my success. Who constantly give me positive energy and help me to fill my cup. Who inject constant love into my life. Even when life is challenging and I have obstacles to overcome, I know I can do it because I believe in myself as much as others believe in me.

I can honestly say I am at my best. I feel well, mentally and physically, and all because I give myself space and time to focus on myself and my wellbeing. To ensure that I nourish my mind, body and soul. I listen to my mind and body and respond by giving them what they actually need, whether this is taking time out or surrounding myself with the people who love me.

The best thing is that every day is full of laughter and smiles. I am enjoying the life I have and making every second count. I give thanks for who I am and what I have become.'

Now I want you to write down in detail everything you saw and imagined whilst you read the passage above using the following lined pages. Write using as much detail as possible. Make what you saw come to life on the page. Don't worry about the order just let the pen do the writing. Write without restriction or limitation. This is your opportunity to design how you want your life to be.

Visualisation

Use these pages to record the life you saw whilst reading the
'My Desired Life'

_____

_____

_____

_____

_____

_____

_____

_____

_____

_____

_____

_____

_____

_____

_____

_____

_____

_____

_____

_____

_____

_____

Are you excited by what you saw?

Do you want what you described?

Of course you do, it's your ideal life. Why wouldn't you?

So why don't you have it now? What is your challenge, blocker, resistance?

Time?

Money?

Energy?

External factors?

Using the following pages, I would like you to take the time to write down and understand:

1. What challenges do you face that are stopping you?
2. What are the blockers that you think are in your way?
3. What resistance do you feel to making that change?

Take the time to work through what you think is stopping you from getting the life you want and ask yourself why until you know the real reason. Then the choice is yours. You can either decide to deal with it or continue as you are. It is that simple.

Use these pages to note your challenges, blockers and resistance.

The truth is, it's easy to find a reason why we cannot and harder to say why we can. It's easier to come up with excuses rather than put on our big girl pants and get on with it. This may seem harsh, but it comes from a place of love. You have the power to overcome anything if you want to. It takes focus, time and compassion. But you can do it. I believe in you.

It's not easy to accept that a lot of the time it's our own excuses that are stopping us. That's why being self-aware is so important. It helps you identify more quickly when you are standing in your own way. When the only one stopping you from moving forward is you. When the fear is holding you back.

And it all comes down to mindset.

The one thing I will always invest in is my mindset. That's time and money. I know that if I've lost my way, I need to take some time to work on my mindset.

It's now time to delve a little deeper. To really understand what you want from work, in your relationships, from your money, for your wellness and the fun stuff.

PART 2

MAKING YOUR
DREAM A REALITY

"Keep smiling, because life is a beautiful thing and there's so much to smile about."

Marilyn Monroe

Let me ask you a simple question, are you living your best life?

As far as I'm concerned, we only get one life. Not only do we get just one but, sorry to break it to you, it's pretty short. So, I don't know about you but I'm trying to make it count.

Now, it's not like I woke up one morning and decided this. It's taken a little while to get to this point. Plus, it takes practice. Continuous practice. And I'm still practising. After all, I'm a regular individual. Some days, life feels easy. However, I still have days when life feels hard. It's at those times when I reflect on where I've come from to decide my next best move.

Like you, I have high moments and low moments. Times when I miss an opportunity and times when I hit a home run. The point is I'm trying my best and that's what counts.

So what does 'living my best life' look like?

For me, it's this:

In my work...

I never intended on starting my own business and now that I'm here I have no intention of going back to being an employee. Well, unless this business really doesn't work and I have no choice. I would never jeopardise my family's security. However, in case you're in any doubt, I don't plan on failing. Even if I have to try one hundred times.

I'm at a point where I enjoy what I'm doing. Yes, there are times when it's a challenge. When I'm not sure where I'm heading and I feel like I'm banging my head against a brick wall, although I'm trying to do things differently. When it feels like all the hard work is getting me nowhere. But I believe this is what I'm supposed to be doing. And that's the point.

If you've managed to get it right, when it comes to work, then it will feel right. It's unlikely that you'll suffer from the Sunday night blues or that Monday morning sinking feeling. The working week will not fill you with dread.

Instead, you look at work with a sense of peace, knowing that you are where you're meant to be and that you're happy with the choice you've made. Even if you've decided that work is just a means to an end and so if it's paying the bills and it funds a good life outside of work then that's good too.

In my relationships...

Relationships are so important to me. Being without my relationships would be like being starved of air. For me, it starts with my family.

My children put everything into perspective. Just watching them can lift my mood when I'm not feeling very motivated. I've learnt to ask 'why not' rather than 'why'! They're also at that age where literally I blink and they've grown ridiculously. I don't want to look back in 20 years and regret not spending enough time with them.

Similarly, without my hubby I wouldn't, firstly, be able to raise our children and, secondly, have been able to start my own business. Yes, I'm my own person. But it's so nice having someone to share life with. Someone who is honest, loving and supportive. Someone who loves me for me, flaws and all.

By now, you'll have realised that I'm all about spending time with family and friends, who I know give me energy and want the best for me. And vice versa. I choose to focus on the ones who fill my cup and who I want to be present with.

I mean, why would you waste time with people who are not your supporters? That just seems crazy. Yes, you may feel obliged. Yes, you may have to. But in all honesty, why would you?

Okay, that might be harsh. So instead, think of it this way: try making a conscious decision on how you manage your relationships. This is your life. So do what's best for you and those you love the most.

I'm more aware of those around me and how I choose to invest my time.

In my money matters...

I learned the value of money from a very young age. Working in my parents' seaside restaurant was the best training ground. It was hard work, but I loved it. And so, since my early twenties, I've consciously managed my money. Whether it's looking for the best deal, investing it wisely or just enjoying it. And I'm now at a point where I know what is possible both in the short term and the long term. I feel financially sorted.

However, for this to carry on I need to actively manage my money and be aware of what is coming in and what is going out. I am mindful that with a growing family, our expenses will increase. We also have a list of experiences we'd like to enjoy, some of which need money.

Things can change in an instant, so managing our money is very important to me.

Money doesn't have to be the limiting factor to living your best life. It's about planning. It's about being creative. It's about knowing what is possible.

In my wellness...

For a long time, I really had no idea. My focus was on making sure that everyone else was okay and on working hard. Physically I was okay, I suppose, although exhausted. Mentally, I was drained. Now I know differently. You can't function on an empty tank.

That's why exercise is so important to me. I love my kickboxing sessions, it gets me moving and helps to focus my mind. I also enjoy being outside, which is just one of the reasons why I run, but it also allows me to vent. It's my opportunity to sort things out in my head whilst exercising and listening to Audible! The added bonus is I feel fighting fit and more than able to keep up with my kids when they want to play.

Then there's my mental wellbeing. Life is busy. There are so many things going on and life could feel more stressful. I need to be strong enough to deal with the pressures of daily life and the curveballs that come my way. So I'm very disciplined when it comes to my mental wellbeing. I practise mindfulness, visualisation and gratitude. And I like a good old natter to release the chatter in my head. However, my go-to is a nightly journal, it really does help me have a better night's sleep.

Looking after my mental wellbeing is about having the opportunity to release my stresses and feel present rather than being bogged down by all the noise of life.

And the fun stuff...

Life wasn't fun for a while. I was stuck on that treadmill. I was locked into a routine and I didn't even know it. All I knew was that I was tired. I was busy but I was just existing, not living.

Life should be fun, so I started to change things. I'm doing more of what I love, spending time with my family and friends, cooking, doing things just for me.

So, I'll say it again. We only get one life so make it count. There's no point in getting to 75 and having regrets. Wishing you did x, y and z. By then it might be too late.

I think Mark Twain put it best, 'Sing like no one's listening, love like you've never been hurt, dance like nobody's watching and live like it's heaven on earth.'

As you read this part of the book, I want you to revisit your designed life from part one to see if you can add to the detail. What Work, Relationships, Wellness, Money Matters and the Fun Stuff mean to you and what you want them to look like.

To help you decide what that might be, within each section of this part of the book you will read about my experiences and thoughts on these five aspects. I want you to use this to trigger your own thoughts and then use the blank pages included after each section to write down, in more detail, what you want as well as the actions and manageable steps you can take to get closer to making your wants reality.

WORK

"You can only become truly accomplished at something you love. Don't make money your goal. Instead pursue the things you love doing and then do them so well that people can't take their eyes off of you."

Maya Angelou

We spend a lot of our time working, so as far as I'm concerned it has to be something that we enjoy. I spent far too long working for Rolls-Royce. I should have followed my gut instinct and left long before I actually did.

But as you know I decided to stay.

I could tell you my 101 excuses for not making the change sooner. Like it wasn't the right time, I didn't know where else to go, I didn't think anyone else would employ me. Or I can just admit that I was comfortable where I was and why change things when all is okay, fine, and it'll do.

The truth is, I'd accepted that every morning I was going to wake up thinking, 'Is this it?' And I had no idea how to change things. So instead of formulating some grand plan and transitioning slowly, which may have been to create a 'side hustle' that would eventually allow me to leave safely, I jumped and just took a leap of faith.

A leap of faith that has paid off.

But what worked for me might not necessarily work for everyone. We are all different. It's finding out what works for you and doing that.

So if you're reading this thinking, I want to change things but I don't know how, then I can help you. You can start by reflecting on what you've learnt from life so far that will help you in the future.

12 THINGS I'VE LEARNT IN BUSINESS THAT ARE LIFE LESSONS

"It's not the mistake that matters, it's how you interpret the lesson."

Michelle C. Ustaszeski

Have you ever been given some advice or been told something important only to say that you already know it?

I have.

The fact is, you don't really know it unless you're doing something with it.

For me, life is one long learning journey, mainly learning from trial and error. It's definitely an emotional way to learn, but because of this association it seems to stay with me, mostly. And because it stays with me, it makes me adapt the way I think, speak and behave.

It's because I want to continuously self-improve and I also have the need to be better and to progress further in life. Something that most of us strive for, but not all of us take seriously.

My biggest opportunities to learn seem to have been since I started my own business. And although I have learnt these lessons since being in business, they are lessons for life.

I'm still learning, but here are my top 12 lessons, some of which you will recognise from earlier in the book.

Being busy is not necessarily a good thing

I was, and still am, so good at being busy. And being busy is good if you're working on the right things. The things that are important and essential. But if being busy is about filling time and space then that's actually counterproductive, leads to productive procrastination and eventually could lead to burnout.

Which has happened to me.

I tend to be so focused on being successful and achieving stuff that I can take on too much at once. The result of which is burnout; feeling sorry for myself, not being able to see the wood from the trees and wanting to give up because it's all too difficult.

One of the most memorable times this happened was in 2018 at Christmas. I'd been so busy, I was exhausted which led to the pendulum swinging the other way. I simply wanted to do nothing! And I couldn't snap out of it. That was until I looked at my children and, in an instant, a switch was flipped. I realised that being numb to life, surrendering and giving up was not good for me and would mean I'd miss out on the fun times with my children.

I'm now more aware of what's really at stake if I find myself being 'busy'.

You either win or learn

Growing up, I was only aware of two options: winning or losing. Being either right or wrong. Succeeding or failing. Not that I was raised thinking that, so I'm not sure why I felt that way. But it's not true. You only lose, are in the wrong or fail if you don't learn. Mistakes and failures are our greatest opportunities to grow, problem solve and find a better way.

I could say my biggest failure was not making Fill That Space, my previous business, a roaring success. But that would be wrong. I learnt so much from running my business and I met amazing people who are still part of my network now. But I have to say that my biggest learning was realising what I really wanted to be doing: 'Mummy on a Break'.

Working hard doesn't always get you what you need

It's not about working hard. It's about working on the right things. Focusing on what is essential and important. If it's neither of these, then it's irrelevant!

This is all about knowing what your priority is and focusing on that. There are limited hours in a day so use them wisely. It's not just about doing, but also taking time out.

My challenge is my magpie tendencies. Remember I love shiny new things. It's so easy for me to say yes to projects that are new and interesting. I'm a starter and not so much a finisher. That's why I'm practising saying no more and being focused on my essentials.

Your biggest challenge is you

The thing that has held me back is me and the thing that will hold you back is you. It's that simple. And how does this happen? It's the thoughts that pop into your head. The thoughts that are neither good nor bad. They're just trying to keep you safe. It's your inner voice.

My inner voice is called Vera. She's this little old lady who just makes me aware of when I'm in 'danger'. When she thinks I might make a mistake, fail or hurt myself. I'm learning to be more aware of Vera and what she thinks. Not to stop her from warning me, but understanding why she's saying what she's saying. I know this may sound crazy but it's insightful and helpful.

You do have a choice. You are free to choose what you do with those thoughts and then take the action that best serves you.

Get out of your comfort zone

It's easy to stay in that place where everything is comfortable and you know what is going on, which is fine until life starts to feel a little bland. Where life has lost its excitement. But it's okay because nothing's rocking the boat and you feel safe.

That's where I was before I left my job back in 2016. Life was good. I had a steady job, we had financial security, everyone was happy. Sort of. I was happy but I was waking up every morning thinking, 'Is this it?' I was missing something. I'd become comfortable. That all changed the minute I decided to start my own business.

I was doing things that I had no clue about. I was learning as I was going. I was just doing my best and I've been uncomfortable ever since, but in a good way.

Just say yes and then make it happen

As I mentioned, I'm like a magpie. I'm attracted to shiny new projects. I love new things and getting involved with new things. I can tell you that when I started my business, I definitely didn't have all the skills I have now.

I had no idea when it came to podcasting, however now not only do I have my own podcast, but I also train others how to do it. I'd never delivered training and now I'm training people regularly on different things. I'd never led a networking group and now I run a very successful networking group full of people who are amazing and who want to help each other progress in their business.

I love it. And all because I said yes, I'll have a go and see what happens.

The one thing I would say is, I would always encourage you to say yes, but only if it is the right thing for you. Does it serve your purpose? Does it align with your goals? Does it contribute to your 'why' in life?

Just do one thing at a time

Life is so much easier when my focus is on one thing at a time, as opposed to trying to multitask. I find that I progress more quickly. I get into the zone, I'm in my flow and I progress further. It's that simple.

Multitasking is a fallacy

If you didn't know, I am a recovering multitasker. I used to think it was great to be able to multitask. Spinning lots of plates at once. Juggling lots of balls. Such a great skill. Very impressive. But is it?

No, no, no. It is stressful. It takes more effort. And things are more likely to go wrong.

Let me paint a picture for you.

I'd be in the kitchen cooking dinner and Lea would want me to help her. I'd stop to help thinking dinner's not going to burn. And whilst helping her with her thing I'd be thinking, 'Oh, I could fold these clothes as well.' So I'm now not even giving my daughter my full attention. Meaning I'd ask her many times to repeat what she was asking me.

The result? She gets annoyed at me because I'm not listening. My ability to fold clothes is worse than a 1 year old doing it. And by the way, dinner will be served well done!

Not only are you doing everything to a substandard, but it takes more effort. Having to pick stuff up and put it down. Trying to remember where you left off. Oh my goodness, it's not worth it.

That's why it's better to do just one thing.

We are all experts at some level

I used to look at my peers and think, oh my goodness, they really know their stuff. One day I'll be like them.

What I've learnt is that we are all experts on our subject, at the point we are at right now. As long as we are one step ahead of the person who is looking to learn then, for now, that is good enough.

It took creating my first workshop, 'How to publish a podcast in 4 easy steps', to see that I have a skill worth sharing. I had the benefit of being the newbie and teaching podcasting in such a way that other newbies could understand what I was saying easily.

Adopt healthy boundaries

I could, if I wanted to, work 24/7. I have lots of ideas and lots of things that I want to do. The problem is, this is not sustainable. Something I found to my detriment, as I've said.

That's why it is important to know what is acceptable and what isn't, then create healthy boundaries to protect yourself. I don't mean build a wall and don't let anyone in. Be sensible about your life and how you want it to look. Then it's important to share these with others, so they know and can respect your boundaries.

If you are new to this, a good place to start would be to have a list of three boundaries you want to put in place and then discuss it with your partner and/or children to see what they think and so they can help you stick to them.

Always acknowledge how far you've come

Running a business sometimes feels like climbing a mountain. It can be hard. It's sometimes scary. And occasionally, I feel like I've started something I can't finish!

That's why it is so important to look backwards. So that in those moments where I'm considering giving up or doubting my ability, I remind myself what I've already accomplished and that I am capable.

You should be your biggest fan

It's great to get a compliment, for others to tell you how great you're doing. However, what if nobody is saying anything, what happens then? Being in business is very challenging and the level of effort I've put into my business is not visible because nobody is with me 24/7. Only I know what I've really done.

That's why it's so important in business and life to be your own head cheerleader. The first one to say how amazing you are regardless of whether you're winning or learning.

This is what has saved me during the dark times. It's me making the decision on what my next best move is. It's me deciding that the pity party is not that much fun and knowing that I can and will turn things around.

NOW IT'S YOUR TURN

Answer these questions using the following lined pages:

1. What have you learnt during your working life?

2. What have you done with that learning?

3. How might it change what work looks like for you today, tomorrow and maybe in a year's time?

FAILURE IS NOT
A SWEARWORD

"You always pass failure on your way to success."

Mickey Rooney

When I worked in the corporate world, making a mistake and failing was not an option. I felt like I had to be two steps ahead of my peers. I had to have the ability to read the minds of my seniors. I felt like I should be the shield between my team and our leaders. Failure was not acceptable.

There's one particular moment in my career where I remember getting a tongue lashing from a director. In his eyes, I was failing and I needed to sort things out. And that was the way things were done back then. This is definitely not acceptable and fortunately I had enough resilience to get on with things. I would say that my experience of managers, in the main, was more stick than carrot, if you know what I mean.

I look back at my time now with wiser eyes and, having experienced the world on my terms, realise how limiting that environment was. Yes, I accept the part I played. But I also acknowledge that it was part of the culture and not just my imagined reality.

The truth is, if we're not careful we can live by the rule in life that 'failure is not an option', which also means accepting the consequences. Living by this rule of not failing puts unnecessary limitations on us. We're accepting that living life means wearing a straightjacket, to stop us from trying anything new in case we fail.

If this were the case, we wouldn't dare to experience new things unless the outcome was certain. We'd always go for the safe option. Personally, that's what I call dull, bland and boring.

Just imagine how different our world would be if the innovators hadn't felt inspired to innovate, just in case they failed! Would we still be living in caves?

So, how often do you practise failing?

I hope the answer is regularly. Is that too much?

When you fail you are being given a great gift: the opportunity to learn, to grow and to try again, but knowing a little more.

But in life, we are conditioned and accept that failing is bad. Failing means we're substandard. It means we're no good and we should give up!

Well, that is nonsense.

The only time failing doesn't serve us is if we don't learn from it and, more importantly, then don't do something with that learning. It's like insisting on banging your head against a brick wall and expecting a different result every time, other than pain!

I actually remember the first time I failed and it really meant something to me. It was my piano exam. It felt horrible. And if that wasn't bad enough, in the same year I failed my clarinet exam as well. I think I was about 10 years old. At that point, I could have just given up and accepted that the universe was trying to tell me something.

But instead, and very maturely, I accepted my failing and consciously tried to understand what went wrong. Why had I not passed? What could I have done differently? I was in middle school at the time, so obviously this was after a period of me stewing and thinking how unfair life was.

Things do go wrong and making mistakes has never been comfortable for me – I'm also a recovering perfectionist by the way – but I'm practising getting used to it. And not only that, I'm finding the positives in every situation as well as learning.

Here is what I've learnt so far:

There is no problem

We have the power to give meaning to the eventual outcome of what we're doing. But the beauty is, we get to decide. Whether you pass or fail, something is only a problem if you decide it's a problem. It could be that you need to take an alternative path.

It's about growing

I like to challenge myself. Try new things. Get involved in new projects. Learn new skills. As it's new, of course, I'm not going to know how to do it from the start. It takes time. I will stumble. I will fall over. But that's part of the learning experience. If we don't try new things, then it's no surprise if we don't progress.

Take imperfect action

I hate making mistakes, but if I waited until everything was just so I would never get out of the starting blocks. It's better to take imperfect action and get moving, than deciding to stand still until everything is in place. By that point the race will have finished and where will you be?

So I'm getting comfortable with taking imperfection action. It might still feel uncomfortable, but with practice it will get better.

Just say yes and try

Life is there to be experienced and I've learnt that sometimes it's a case of just saying yes and then figuring out the how. Plus saying yes and knowing there is a deadline, is the motivation I need to move things on. Becoming stuck by the fear of failure and the unknown is paralysing. Saying yes to opportunities can be scary but also liberating.

Trial and error are best

What has stayed with me more often than not is when something has not gone according to plan and I've made mistakes. I've learnt the most from these events and because of it, I've come back with something even better the next time. It's a great way to learn, even if it feels uncomfortable at the time.

I encourage you to be brave and say yes to failure. Say yes to trying new things, to see where it will take you. And to say yes to learning and growing. The world is waiting for you to experience it.

I invite you to embrace failure and instead of working against it, work with it.

NOW IT'S YOUR TURN

Answer these questions using the following lined pages:

1. Do you know where your next failure is?
2. When you're thinking about your work and your career, are you staying safe?
3. Are you choosing to stay safe and stick to what you know?
4. How would it feel to pause and decide what you really want?
5. Do you have the courage to make the change that is right for you?

RETURNING TO WORK AFTER MATERNITY LEAVE DOESN'T HAVE TO SUCK

"A year from now you may wish you had started today."

Karen Lamb

Before I went on maternity leave, I enjoyed going to work. I knew what I was doing. All the information I needed was neatly stored in my head. I could recall everything and anything I needed.

I was super confident in myself and my work.

So I thought returning to work after maternity leave would be easy.

This was not the case. It felt alien to me, I felt like a fish out of water. I couldn't remember half the things I used to. Plus things had changed, time had moved on and I hadn't been part of it.

I remember asking my manager when he expected me to be performing like before. Fortunately, he was supportive and told me to take one day at a time. Great advice, but this didn't stop me from feeling frustrated. I wanted to be how I was before. I'm not very good at being patient.

The truth is, not all new mums have a good experience returning to work. Whether it's because their manager is not supportive, or their colleagues just don't understand or it's the good old inner critic telling them they can't.

If you're at the point of returning to work, or maybe you've already returned to work, and it doesn't feel right, then I can tell you it doesn't have to be this way. You don't have to feel alone.

To be honest, I do remember being a little excited about going back to work. Mainly because I could have some me-time. I could be Maria instead of Lea's mummy. I could concentrate on what was going on in my world instead of cleaning, cooking and childcare.

But I was also anxious. Whilst I was on maternity leave the world hadn't stopped. Things had moved on in work and all without me.

The thing is, I hadn't stopped to think about what returning to work meant for me. What I wanted from my work and how I wanted to transition back to work.

To say day one was a blur is an understatement.

My colleagues asked about my daughter and what it was like being a mum, but I felt like I was having an out of body experience. This place was familiar. The people were the same. But at the same time, it all felt very different and surreal.

I wanted to just get on with work. Why couldn't I just get on with work? I felt stuck. It was like I was the new girl again. Which would have been fine if I was. But I was just returning to work and the job I had before.

I felt like I really had no idea.

Fast forward to now and I love my work. Yes, I'm doing something completely different but it's what I'm meant to be doing. I work with amazing women who are trying to do their best for themselves whilst raising a family. I help them to help themselves get to where they want to go. Not only do these women feel better, but the ripple effect is that everyone else around will also feel the benefit.

But as I've said, life wasn't always like this. When I first became a mum and I was trying to transition back to work, it felt more like a slap in the face.

Before maternity leave, I was a confident project manager dealing with all types of people, from the intense 'tell it how it is' production workers to the more tactful 'it has to be right' engineers.

I was confident because I knew my stuff. I knew what was going on. I knew what needed to be done.

But when I returned to work, I felt the opposite.

If I knew then what I know now I would have done things differently. Starting with…

Talking to other mums who had already returned to work

The only way to understand what it can look and feel like, is to have a good old chat with someone who has already been there. To talk to someone who is walking in your shoes already, be honest about what you're feeling and for them to tell you it will be okay and give you advice.

Prepare, prepare, prepare

There's nothing better than being prepared. It's not just for girl guides! This is not just knowing what the law says about returning to work, it's also understanding what you want. What does work mean to you now? It might be the same as before or it might be different. It's so important to know what your needs and wants are first, then you can actually tell whoever needs to know so they are better equipped to help.

Talk to your manager before you return to work

Whether you have a supportive manager or not, it's helpful to understand where they're coming from and how they plan on supporting you in coming back to work. Plus, you get the opportunity to tell them what you want and how they can help.

Get ready mentally

It's so important to look after your mental wellbeing as you navigate working now that you're a mum. Practise mindfulness or meditation, or maybe something a little more vigorous like running or punching a punchbag. Whatever helps you to come to terms and get comfortable with going back to work.

Buy your back to work outfit

It may sound superficial but looking good on the outside will help with feeling good on the inside. Whether it's putting together an outfit from clothes that you already have or buying something new. Feeling good with what you're wearing will really help.

Hindsight is a wonderful thing and can teach us a lot regardless of what the situation is. Whether you're returning to work or about to try something new, it's great to look back at what you've been through to see how it can help in the future.

You are not the person you used to be, however by doing a couple of things up front you can be more confident in returning to work, knowing what you want and who you are now.

NOW IT'S YOUR TURN

Answer these questions using the following lined pages:

1. How are you planning on returning to work?

2. Have you already returned to work and are finding it a little awkward?

3. Do you find yourself daydreaming about doing something different?

HOW TO IDENTIFY

YOUR SUPERPOWER

"The things that make us different, those are our

superpowers."

Lena Waithe

Being a mum, I know I have superpowers. I can recollect where anything was last left, especially as my kids regularly expect me to know. I have amazing hearing which is so valuable as not only can I answer my family's questions immediately when they ask, but I also know what's happening in any part of the house and whether I need to get involved. And I am an expert when it comes to juggling tasks like cooking, playing with my kids and sorting out technical issues. Although, as you know, I'm unlearning this one!

That's all great, but that's not what I mean.

We all have superpowers. Superpowers that seek to serve us and superpowers that we use to serve others. But what is a superpower?

A superpower is a skill or knowledge that comes easily to us. Some people also call it the zone of genius. We are so good at it that, to us, we wouldn't think of it as a superpower. Whereas for someone else, it's impressive and brings great value when we share it.

The great thing about knowing what your superpower is, if you choose to, it could become your work. Your new career. Or maybe just something that gives you pleasure every day and that is your escape from the chaos of the world.

Intrigued to find out what your superpower is? Here are six tips to help you identify it:

Find some time

This may seem obvious, but to go through the process of identifying your superpower, you actually need to put aside some time to think about it. Some time when you know you can focus and you won't be disturbed.

Create the right environment

To allow your creativity to flow, it's important to create the right environment. Put on some inspiring music, maybe light a candle, use your favourite pen to write with and sit in a cosy corner. Whatever you need to get you into the zone.

Get creative

With a pen in hand, list everything you can do, such as things that you love and have a passion for and skills and knowledge that you will have acquired throughout your life. Notice when people may have remarked about how well you do something or how easy you made something. Just write down everything as it comes to you. Don't think about an order or how to write it. Just write.

Patterns and themes

Look at your list and notice whether there are any patterns or recurring themes. Does anything jump out at you? Does anything surprise you? Can you see what your superpowers are?

Notice your feelings

Notice how you feel now that you know you do have superpowers. Which ones make you feel excited? Which ones put a smile on your face?

How could you make more use of your superpower?

Superpowers have little value unless you're using them. So the question is, what will you do with your superpower? How can you get the most out of it? How can you share it with others?

It's great to identify what you're good at, especially if you love it and you have a passion for it. It's even better if you can share it.

NOW IT'S YOUR TURN

Answer these questions using the following lined pages:

1. Now that you know what your superpower is, what will you do with it?
2. Do you want to share it?
3. Is it something that could make you extra money?
4. Would you like it to be your new career?

Use this page to note your thoughts, assumptions and aspirations for your desired work.

Use this page to note the actions you will take to progress the changes you want to make in your work.

_____

_____

_____

_____

_____

_____

_____

_____

_____

_____

_____

_____

_____

_____

_____

_____

_____

_____

_____

_____

_____

_____

_____

_____

RELATIONSHIPS

"I don't need anyone to rectify my existence. The most profound relationship we will ever have is the one with ourselves."

Shirley MacLaine

Human beings are social beings. We feel the need to be with other people. We feel safe when we are with other people. It's all about belonging to a group that will support us.

However, our need to be part of a tribe has changed. No longer do we need to be part of a tribe for our survival. The world outside our front door is not as dangerous as it once was. Yet, we haven't been able to shake that need to be accepted, to be part of a 'family'.

To be accepted means to be the same and hide any differences we have, all of which is exhausting.

Is our only option to fit in? To be the same? To stay silent in case we rock the boat? To continue to wear a mask in case your true identity is unacceptable?

The choice is yours.

What would it feel like to drop the mask that protects you?

To be 100 per cent you and live compassionately as well as to show compassion to others?

You may stumble at first, but it would become easy with practice.

Don Miguel says, 'Be impeccable with your word.' Which means to speak your truth with your whole being and not just words. However, it also means to be aware of the impact your truth has on others and to speak with love.

Looking at all the relationships in your life, are you being impeccable with your word? Are you speaking your truth? Do you speak with love?

ARE YOU GETTING THE MOST OUT OF YOUR RELATIONSHIPS?

"When we love, we always strive to become better than we are. When we strive to become better than we are, everything around us becomes better too."

Paulo Coehlo

We have so many different types of relationships in our lives. Family, friends, partners, children, work, etc. Some that build us up and others that drain us of energy and are hard work. The good ones fill us with love, joy and happiness. The not so good ones bring us down and drain our energy.

I want to fill my life with the relationships that make me happy. Life is too short and time is too precious, so my focus is on the ones that fill my heart with joy.

The thing is, we can't change people and it's not up to us to change people. But we are fully in control of our behaviour, the way we react and the decisions we make. For me, it's about how we manage relationships.

I have lots of different relationships in my life. There's my hubby, my kiddies, my family, my friends and my work colleagues. Each one is different and each one gives me something different. For a long time, I accepted them for what they were. However, if I want to really enjoy my relationships and give and get the most out of them, it's more than that.

It's about:

- Knowing why I'm in this relationship
- Understanding what the relationship means to me
- Understanding the individuals I have relationships with
- Acknowledging the changes in our lives

These are questions that we don't always consider consciously but for me, it's become really important.

This has made things a lot clearer for me. I feel generally more relaxed. I can enjoy spending time with people I can truly be me around. And so, it all starts with you.

Things to consider

I've taken time to think about what I want my relationships to look like. How I want them to make me feel and what I want to give to my relationships. This is especially true with my kids. They are two very assertive, funny children. I want our household to be calm and fun, which is easy when everyone is calm and fun.

But what about the times when things become hectic? Or when time is against us and we need to move quickly? Or when one of them is throwing a tantrum? Not so easy. This is where I need to remain calm. Again, not so easy. Trying to battle with them is hard work. And you can't reason with children who are fired up.

For me, the relationship with my children is all about love. This doesn't mean that I'm a pushover when things are tough. I still stand my ground. I remain consistent. I remind them that I love them. Trust me, they calm down a lot more quickly than when it turns into a battle of wills.

People change

We are not the same person we were 5, 10 or 20 years ago. Priorities change. Situations change. And as a result, relationships change. You may find that people drift away and you have less in common with people. This is only natural.

There is a well-known poem written by someone anonymous that describes how people are in your life for either a season, reason or lifetime. I believe in this. And yes, it is sad when we lose touch with people or something changes. But it's part of life.

Obligations

There are some people that you have to have in your life. Maybe a family member. Maybe a work colleague. For me, this is about acknowledging their presence, being respectful and polite, knowing what my boundaries are and not taking anything personally.

Glass half empty

What about the friend that always sees life as negative? Well, this is a very personal decision. Do you minimise contact? Do you cut them out of your life? I know that's a bit harsh. It's up to you. Firstly, what are you comfortable with? Secondly, how would they feel?

Relationships are so important in my life. I'd find it hard to believe that anyone can exist without relationships, although I know there are people in this world who choose to live a life of solitude.

Don't get me wrong, I'm quite happy with my own company but I'm even happier when I'm with people. People who I admire, love or inspire me. This may be because I'm a Taurean. It may come from my Greek heritage. But the fact is, I love good company and I cherish all my relationships.

NOW IT'S YOUR TURN

Answer these questions using the following lined pages:

1. What about your relationships:

2. How do they make you feel?

3. Do you find that your behaviour changes depending on who you're with?

4. Are you able to be just you?

5. Are you being a role model to others?

ARE YOU A GOOD ROLE MODEL?

"Be the role model you needed when you were younger."

Anonymous

When I was younger, I wanted to be like my dad. He was, and still is, a force to be reckoned with. I admired his drive and passion for life. The fact that he'd want to make things happen, no matter what the obstacles or challenges were.

Then I became a mum. It was at that point that I truly understood what my mum had done, and still does, for us. I didn't have to aspire to be like her, because the way she'd raised us meant that I was already like her. I'd already picked up from her what it meant to be a mum and what that looked and sounded like.

What I'm trying to say is, I aspire to take all the good things from my parents and learn from their experiences to be the best I can be, so that I can be a good role model to my children.

One pretty obvious thing is that if I'm going to be a good role model to my children, for me, it takes more than words. I want to actively show my children through my actions.

What do I mean?

It's all very well wanting the best for your kids. Encouraging them to follow their dreams. Supporting them through the ups and downs. However, if you're not doing that for yourself then what message are you really sending?

Your actions and words must be the same, otherwise aren't your words meaningless?

For me, this started by leaving my corporate career of 17 years and deciding what I really wanted to do in life. And as you know, so much more has happened since.

Here are my five tips for being a good role model:

Lead by example

How can we expect anyone to take us seriously, especially our children, if we're not following our own advice? Why should we expect anyone to do what we say if we're not doing it ourselves?

I believe quite strongly in leading by example. It's about not just talking, and giving out a lot of hot air, but actually getting on and doing it.

Do what you said you'd do

This is simple to do and yet easier not to do. For me, it's about trust. How can we expect anyone to trust us if we don't do what we say we'd do? Just imagine how much better the world would be if everyone just did what they said they'd do.

It's also about managing expectations, especially when it comes to our children. I know my children take what I say literally. And why shouldn't they? If I was to regularly go against what I'd said or not see through what I'd said, then I shouldn't be surprised if they no longer believe me and so distrust the words I'm saying.

Be honest

Not just in the words you use but also in being able to admit when you've made a mistake or done something wrong. We are only human, not superhuman. We make mistakes, which isn't necessarily a bad thing. It also takes courage to admit when you've made a mistake, but people tend to respect you more if you're able to admit it.

So be honest.

Do your best

The most we expect of anyone is that they'll do their best, knowing that this will differ depending on how they're feeling on that day. Just think of all the things that could be accomplished if we just did our best.

Be kind to yourself

Everything we do starts with ourselves, which also means being kind to ourselves. Life can be hectic. Life throws us curve balls. Life sometimes just doesn't work out how we expected. But being kind to ourselves makes these bumps and knocks easier to manage. If everyone was kind, life would be a lot nicer.

Being a good role model is quite simple. It's making a choice about how we behave, how we respond, how we choose to act and how we speak.

NOW IT'S YOUR TURN

Answer these questions using the following lined pages:

1. How are you a good role model?

2. How are you leading by example?

3. Are you being the best you can be?

Use this page to note your thoughts, assumptions and aspirations about your relationships.

_____

_____

_____

_____

_____

_____

_____

_____

_____

_____

_____

_____

_____

_____

_____

_____

_____

_____

_____

_____

_____

_____

_____

_____

Use this page to note the actions you will take to improve your relationships.

_____

_____

_____

_____

_____

_____

_____

_____

_____

_____

_____

_____

_____

_____

_____

_____

_____

_____

_____

_____

_____

_____

_____

MONEY MATTERS

"It's not how much money you make, but how much money you keep, how hard it works for you, and how many generations you keep it for."

Robert Kiyosaki

Money is not evil and to want money is not greedy. We need money to live. To buy the basics so we have food, clothing and shelter. It is the currency that we use in today's modern society.

However, money is often seen as a bad thing. Whether you think that anyone who has lots of money is bad or that money is the root of all evil, these are actually stories that we have heard and they have become part of our belief system.

The key is to understand how you feel and think about money, as this will unlock many of the blockers you have and will help you to heal your relationship with money.

Whether you're a spender, a saver or somewhere in between, we all have an opinion about money, which defines the relationship we have with it. Money doesn't have to be the enemy.

# DOES MONEY MATTER?

*"Money isn't everything...but it ranks right up there
with oxygen."*

Rita Davenport

I've always been money conscious. I guess it comes from my parents. They
may have moved to the UK for different reasons and at different times, but
they were starting again and had nothing. And so, my childhood definitely
included learning and understanding the value of money.

Being a child whose parents owned a seaside restaurant meant that my
weekend, after school and summer job was working in the restaurant. And
it was no easy ride. All of us worked in the family business, which included
my brother and sister. We didn't have pocket money, we had wages. It was
my money and I worked hard for it. So, I was very protective of what I did
with it.

This is the same today. When it comes to money, for me, it's a serious
matter. I want to know that I'm in control of the here and now as well as
the future. I don't want to worry about money. It's true what they say: look
after the pennies and the pounds will look after themselves.

Don't get me wrong, this doesn't mean I don't spend money. Life is not free. Living is not free. Experiencing life is not free. And I love life, so I do spend. I simply ensure that I'm organised and I look for smart ways to use my money.

Let me show you.

The here and now

Budgeting. Yes, I know not the most exciting subject but it's the key to our daily living. If you don't know how much your basic cost of living is, then how do you know you're getting the most value from your pennies? How do you know that you're not wasting money?

Think of yourself as a mini business. You are the director of your household. In an ideal world, money coming in would be more than money going out, giving you space to save and invest for the future.

Personally, I don't like borrowing money unless it's for a mortgage. So, we live within our means and I know the cost of all our household bills. Yes, I like to be in control. Which means I know what surplus we have every month. This means I know how much we have to spend on the nice things like holidays, meals out and day trips.

Doing things differently

This is about minimising unnecessary costs and looking for alternative ways of getting the most from our money. It's not about thinking there's a lack of money. It's just making a conscious decision on how to spend it in the best way. Let me give you a few examples:

- Meals out versus a packed lunch – when we go on a day trip, I'll make up a simple picnic instead of eating out.

- Annual membership – we are members of the National Trust and so we have plenty of day trip opportunities which work out being a lot cheaper.

- Vouchers and discount codes – I try, where possible, to find a voucher or discount code when I need to buy something.

- Buying things in the sale – taking advantage of the sales may be tedious but you can find a bargain.

The future

It may seem like a long way off, but it's closer than you think. For me, it's about peace of mind. I want to know that I'm able to give my family what they need in the future. The sooner I start planning for it, the more likely that it will be possible.

I don't know what will happen in the future, but I know what I want to make allowances for, including:

- My children wanting to go to university
- My children wanting to get married
- My children wanting to buy a house
- Travelling around the world with hubby
- Funding my retirement

It's amazing what a little bit of planning can achieve. Unless you're just putting it off and hoping that at that point in the future, when you need money, miracles will happen.

NOW IT'S YOUR TURN

Answer these questions using the following lined pages:

1. Do you know what your money situation is?

2. Are you in control of your finances?

3. Are you making the most out of your money?

Use this page to note your thoughts, assumptions and aspirations about your money.

Use this page to note the actions you will take to improve your relationship with money and what actions you will take to improve your money matters.

_____

_____

_____

_____

_____

_____

_____

_____

_____

_____

_____

_____

_____

_____

_____

_____

_____

_____

_____

_____

_____

_____

_____

≫WELLNESS≪

"Take care of your body, it's the only place you have to live."

Jim Rohn

The only person responsible for our wellbeing is us. Yes, there are lots of external forces that will poke and prod us, but this only emphasises how important it is to look after ourselves.

As I've said many times, our bodies are very clever and a simple ache and pain is more than a simple ache or pain, it is our body's way of communicating with us. Telling us that something needs attention.

A friend of mine has a very simple phrase which is, 'Listen to your body whisper before it starts to shout.'

So instead of getting to the point that your body is continuously whispering and is maybe on the verge of shouting, do something now.

Build into your weekly routine activities that support your life as well as your wellbeing. It doesn't just have to be about you, get your family involved.

THE ANSWERS TO EVERYTHING YOU NEED ARE WITHIN YOU

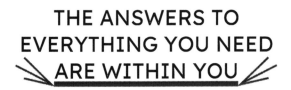

"Changing your mindset may change the situation."

Lisa Rusczyk

If something is not going the way you expected it to, what do you do?

The answer is not to work harder.

The answer is not to work longer.

The answer is not to do more.

Our default is to do more, however, what if the answer was to do less?

I invite you to try an alternative.

I invite you to stop and take the time to think.

I invite you to pause so you can understand what is going on.

I invite you to breathe so you can be grounded in the here and now.

We spend a lot of our time with our heads down being busy with the doing, when in fact stopping can be more productive. We associate progress with taking action. We think that the only way we can move forward is if we physically do something.

But that's not the case.

You know I am a doer. I like to be busy and get things done. But that doesn't always help me. Sometimes what I really need is to stop and think. To regain my perspective. To take a minute so I can decide on my next best move. Which may be to do nothing. To be still. I know this all sounds very 'alternative'.

When things seem to go wrong or not according to plan, it triggers us. We start to feel bad and start to wonder why. We go searching for answers in the external world.

What I really want to say is, you already have the answers. The only person who is going to make you feel better is you. Not other people, products or experiences.

Sure, looking for an answer in external places can make you feel good for a time, but it's temporary. And when it goes, you'll be looking to get your fix again.

As humans, we look to the external world to make us happy. To make us feel better when our life appears to not be what we want it to be.

As humans, we look for instant gratification. Whether that's getting a compliment from someone, waiting for your social media post to go viral or even winning the lottery.

Just like a craving, we're looking for a fix. And worse than that, over time, we look for a bigger fix. To the point where nothing will satisfy the craving because it's become too big!

However, what if you could satisfy that craving? What if, instead of looking to get that fix from others you just look to yourself? The truth is, the road to happiness starts from within and knowing who you are.

It starts with letting go of all the things that you think are you, being completely honest with yourself and allowing yourself to understand who you really are. With looking inwards, to be comfortable being you. It just starts with you.

Wouldn't that make life easy?

Wouldn't that relieve the stress?

Wouldn't that bring about calm?

It's about looking after yourself and your wellness, which means mentally and physically.

I invite you to try the following:

Listen to your body

If only we properly listened to ourselves, life would feel so much easier. The body knows what it wants and what it needs. By listening and getting curious, you will understand better what is going on for you.

Let go of the past

Our past stops us from moving forward. The experiences we've had, the conversations we have, the people we've met. And without knowing it, we hold on to the negative ones more tightly which then define our reality and stop us from seeing what is right in front of us.

Acknowledge your gifts

We all have gifts. Skills and abilities that we're good at. Yet we tend to focus on what we're not good at. I invite you to acknowledge all your gifts and focus on making good use of them.

Be in the present

What really matters is now. The past has happened and cannot be altered. The future is yet to happen. The only time we have is now. So instead of being distracted by what happened and what might be, embrace where you are now.

Stop making excuses

You are the only person who is standing in your way. Nobody can force us to do or not do something. We have a choice, even if we don't think we have. And when we think we don't have any options, that's when you know you are making excuses.

Taking the time to work on yourself and to understand who you are and what you want is your next best move and will give the answers you are looking for.

It's about creating a strong mindset and focusing on your wellbeing, so you are so comfortable in your own skin that you can and will achieve anything. Plus, you'll be the best you can be which means that not only will you benefit but your loved ones will too.

It starts now.

NOW IT'S YOUR TURN

Answer these questions using the following lined pages:

1. Are you listening to your body?
2. What are you doing to let go of the things you think are holding you back?
3. What can you do to remain in the present?
4. What would it take to spend time focused on your wellness?
5. How can you accept you for you?

I ACCEPT ME,  FLAWS AND ALL

"I realized that I don't have to be perfect. All I have to do is show up and enjoy the messy, imperfect and beautiful journey of my life."

Kerry Washington

When you look in the mirror do you like who you see looking back? Or are you far too busy noticing any imperfections?

It might be what you physically look like, the shape of your eyebrows, the size of your ears or the way your hair falls.

It might be deeper than that. It could be in the way you sometimes behave or the things you might say or how you feel about certain things.

Or it might be the way you talk to yourself!

What would happen if you learned to love the things you don't like? What would happen if you fully embraced the things you don't like? What if you could see the positives in what you see as flaws?

You would see how unique you are, how amazing you are. You would see all the pieces of the jigsaw puzzle that make you who you really are. You would see the whole you.

It's taken me a long time to fully embrace my flaws. And to be honest, it's a daily practice. But it's been a really important journey for me, which all started with me saying yes to a mindset coach.

I want to be the best I can be and having flaws just felt like they were stopping me from getting to where I wanted to go. But the truth is my flaws are a part of what makes me, me.

Can you imagine a world in which we were all flawless? Oh my goodness, how dull that would be and even a little scary!

So, I'm learning to love my flaws. I'm learning to be okay with not being okay. I'm learning to be 100 per cent me.

You're not broken and you don't need fixing. You just need to embrace who you are, flaws and all.

Here are five tips to help you love who you are, flaws and all:

Reconnect

We are constantly changing and it's easy to not recognise who we have become. So take the time to reconnect with who you really are. What do you like? What makes you laugh? What are you about?

Values

It starts with understanding what your values are and what values are important to you. Knowing your values helps you to make decisions and take action. When we make a decision or take action that is in alignment with our values, life flows in the right way for us. Life becomes easy.

Do things that make you laugh and smile

Life is about having fun. It's about being able to laugh at yourself and with yourself. So do things that put a smile on your face. Allow yourself to be carefree. If you don't know what that is then reflect on your childhood for a clue. If that doesn't help then ask a child. They may not know the answer but hearing their opinion will make you smile.

Gratitude

Write a list of ten things you are grateful for. This will remind you of what is important to you. Then it's up to you to ensure you have more of it in your life.

Me-time

As I've said before, you are the lead actor in your life, so if you're not giving yourself some time and space to just be then you've demoted yourself to a supporting role. Is that what you want? It's about giving yourself the time to accept who you are. Because you are unique, you are enough and you're worth it.

If you need it, I'm giving you permission to accept all of you, flaws and all. I invest in myself so why wouldn't you.

NOW IT'S YOUR TURN

Answer these questions using the following lined pages:

1. What will it take for you to accept all of you, flaws and all?

2. How would it feel to love the person looking back at you in the mirror?

3. What would it take for you to acknowledge how amazing you are?

7 TIPS TO KEEPING YOUR IDENTITY WHEN YOU'RE A MUM

"Mother is a verb. It's something you do. Not just who you are."

Cheryl Lacey Donovan

When I became a mum, I automatically put myself at the bottom of the list. My priorities changed. The needs of my children came first followed by hubby. It wasn't a conscious decision. It was automatic. I suppose my need to look after others was stronger than the need to look after myself.

The thing is, we are all individuals and we are not defined by the roles we play. Keeping your identity rests in your hands. You define you. No one else. By doing just a few simple things, you can give yourself space and time to ensure you're not at the bottom of the list.

Whether you're new to the world of being a mum or you're a seasoned veteran, here are my seven tips for keeping your identity.

Introduce yourself

Always introduce yourself as who you are and then your child's name when meeting other parents.

I don't think I even realised I was doing it, but my default would be to introduce myself as Lea or Louka's mummy and then say my name. Sometimes I would even forget to say my name, which really doesn't help.

Make time for yourself to do things you want

It's so easy to forget to do things you like and want to do when you have children. My focus is usually on making sure they're getting the best experiences and they have things to do. But it is just as important that I also have time to do what I want to do.

This may mean waiting until the evening when you think you're exhausted. But if that's the only time you have then make it count.

Have me-time

I remember that there didn't feel like there was enough time to have me-time. There was always something to do. There's still always something to do. The thing is, everyone else seems to have their own time.

Me-time doesn't have to be anything fancy like getting a facial or having a massage, although I do like a facial once and a while. It can be just going for a walk. It's free and it's easy to do.

Dress yourself for you

When I first became a mum, I dressed to be practical. My first thought would be, what should I wear to make breastfeeding easy? Followed by what would hide any baby related stains, followed by what's comfortable.

Whereas before children, I enjoyed clothes more. Don't get me wrong, I wasn't a Fashionista. But I dressed how I wanted to dress. And there is no reason why this shouldn't be the same when you're a mum. Yes, there have to be some adjustments, but nothing that can't be managed.

Keep your brain active

The company of little people becomes the norm, which is great. I loved going to baby groups. I loved spending time with my babies. But this is not great for your brain. Your brain is like a muscle and it needs to be exercised.

Whether this is reading, doing sudoku or attempting a 1000 piece jigsaw puzzle, keep using your brain.

Don't forget your pre-mummy self

Becoming a mum doesn't mean retiring your old self. There may be bits that no longer have a role in your life but there will be parts that should remain.

For me, it's important to stay in touch with my friends. Friends who really know me and who really get me. Some are close and so I get to meet up with them for dinner or coffee. Others live further away, and so meeting up is less frequent and those relationships rely more on texts.

You are unique

We are all unique. Just because we're now mums doesn't make us the same, although we do have things in common. We have led different lives. We don't necessarily share the same principles.

It's not about fitting in, it's about just being you. Whatever that means.

Being a mum is an awesome thing. It's a role that I have embraced, but I've also fought to retain my identity. To know who I am no matter what role I'm playing. So remember, you are also an individual who matters.

NOW IT'S YOUR TURN

Answer these questions using the following lined pages:

1. What are you doing to keep your identity?
2. How are you ensuring that you embrace you as an individual?
3. What would it take to just be you, instead of always a mummy?

Use this page to note your thoughts, assumptions and
aspirations about your wellness.

_____

_____

_____

_____

_____

_____

_____

_____

_____

_____

_____

_____

_____

_____

_____

_____

_____

_____

_____

_____

_____

_____

_____

_____

Use this page to note the actions you will take to improve your wellness.

_____

_____

_____

_____

_____

_____

_____

_____

_____

_____

_____

_____

_____

_____

_____

_____

_____

_____

_____

_____

_____

_____

_____

_____

 FUN STUFF

"Don't take life too seriously! Nobody gets out alive anyway. Smile. Be goofy. Take chances. Have fun. Inspire."

Dawn Gluskin

If you're not having fun, then what are you doing? Maybe living on autopilot. Maybe the thought of having fun hasn't crossed your mind. Maybe, even worse than that, you're blaming others.

That's your cue to stop.

Pause.

Reflect.

Then decide.

What does fun mean to you?

How can you bring the fun back into your life?

What is your next best move?

How can you bring others on board?

Yes, life has its serious moments but life is there to be enjoyed. So if you're not having fun then what are you doing?

DON'T FORGET THE
FUN STUFF

"If you obey all the rules, you miss all the fun."

Katherine Hepburn

Do you ever wonder where children get their energy from? It doesn't matter what time of day it is, my kiddies always have bags of energy. Well, except for when we're on our way back from a family day trip and the car motion has gently rocked them to sleep. Then, without fail, as soon as we're back home they spring into life.

My explanation is that they have a zest for life. They want to take advantage of every waking hour. They haven't got the baggage that adults have. There isn't that voice inside their heads telling them that they're tired.

As a mum to two young children, for a while I was listening to that tired voice.

My day would start with me dragging myself out of bed, not quite ready to get up. I would then sometimes go through the day in a trance, helping myself to the odd caffeine loaded coffee to help me wake up. After a hard day's work, the kiddies would then come home bouncing off the walls. Full of high spirits, wanting to play before their wind down. So, by the time they were in bed I was nearly ready to also go to bed, exhausted from the day's activities. Instead of giving in, I'd just be slumped on the sofa, gormlessly watching television until it was a reasonable time to actually go to bed!

But this all changed at the end of 2018.

It wasn't a lightning bolt. It was gradually building up over a few months. I realised that although I'd got off the corporate bus I still felt like a slave to the treadmill of life. I realised that I wanted to make more changes.

By getting off the corporate bus, I'd made the first step, which was to take back control. But that wasn't enough. I'd changed just one element of my life. The practical part. The serious part, my work. But what about making life fun? What about having fun? My children and husband are my priorities, but it's also about putting me first.

What am I going on about?

Doing the things that make you happy. Doing the things that are just for you. Remember, this is about you the individual, not you in your other roles. Not the mum, the wife, the worker. Just you. It's not being selfish. It's you looking after you in the same way you look after others.

But where to start?

If you don't know what the fun stuff is for you then the best place to start is your childhood. What were the things you enjoyed doing as a child? What were your hobbies and interests? Or there might be new things you want to try. Now's the time. Go for it.

But I'm too tired.

I used to think I was too tired. I'd look at hubby and I was envious that he still had the energy to do stuff that he enjoyed once we put the kiddies to bed. I wondered why he wasn't as tired as me. It's really quite simple, if you're doing something you enjoy you will not feel too tired. Even now he'll stay up until the early morning to get that perfect night-time shot of the stars and the moon.

What am I doing about it?

I had a bit of a revelation. The things that were missing, actually energised me once I brought them back into my life.

I love music. Whether it's playing a tune on the piano, singing along to some cheesy tunes, dancing like nobody's watching or just listening to my favourite tracks. It's a great way of relieving stress, letting out my emotions and simply having fun.

I enjoy spending time with friends and family. Arranging coffee catch ups or family day trips. I love the company of others.

I need to exercise. I regularly go for a run. I also train twice a week for kickboxing. It's a great way to start the day and a great way to wind down the day. It's a great way to focus on the here and now and drown out the noise of the day.

And finally, I love food. I'm in danger of repeating myself but I love eating it, cooking it and talking about it. I'm a home cook who loves to feed people. That's how I show love.

It's up to me to bring the fun stuff into my life. I could just go through the motions. I could just make sure that everyone else is okay.

But how would that make me feel?

At this point, I need to point out that this doesn't mean that every day is full of joy. I'm a human too. There are days when, frankly, fun is at the bottom of my list. The point I'm trying to make is that I'm now making a conscious decision to do something. That's the difference. No more excuses. No waiting for someone to change things. I'm changing things. After all, it's in my hands.

NOW IT'S YOUR TURN

Answer these questions using the following lined pages:

1. How are you bringing back the fun into your life?

2. What do you need to do to put a smile on your face?

3. What would it take to make life feel fun?

Use this page to note your thoughts, assumptions and
aspirations about bringing fun into your life.

Use this page to note the actions you will take to have more fun.

_____
_____
_____
_____
_____
_____
_____
_____
_____
_____
_____
_____
_____
_____
_____
_____
_____
_____
_____
_____
_____
_____
_____

PART 3

CRUSHING THE CHALLENGES THAT WILL GET IN YOUR WAY

"You gain strength, courage and confidence by every experience in which you really stop to look fear in the face. You must do the thing you think you cannot do."

Eleanor Roosevelt

It is now your turn to make the changes that you know are right for you, but up until now you may not have had the courage to do. I'm here to tell you that it just starts with one step. Your first step. It doesn't have to be difficult. You can make it simple. It just takes commitment from you to start and then to keep going until life is what you want to be.

There will be times when you stumble and fall. That's to be expected. It's at that point that you get up, dust yourself off and decide your next best move. There will also be many times when you'll achieve things you never thought were possible. This is the time to celebrate and acknowledge how far you've come.

You know you are entitled to live the life you want. It's not selfish and there is no need to feel guilty. However, I know that these words may not be enough to encourage you to take action. So, I'd like to share some more words of wisdom with you. To show you that it is okay and you can do it.

The only person who has the power to change your life as you know it is you. So let me ask you, what will it take for you to decide to do something different now? To stop living life on autopilot, or feel like you are sleepwalking through life.

ARE YOU SLEEPWALKING THROUGH LIFE?

"All our dreams can come true – if we have the courage to pursue them."

Walt Disney

Do you feel like you're sleepwalking through life?

It's easy to get swept along with life. To go on autopilot. And how does that make you feel?

Numb? Indifferent? Out of touch?

It's as though you're living life in a trance. Or just going through the motions of your daily routine. Maybe it's all about adhering to the demands of the day.

Oh my goodness, that feels heavy! I know that feeling well.

I would say I was sleepwalking through life when I first became a mum, not just because of the lack of sleep. Obviously, life had changed completely. I went from doing what I wanted when I wanted, to being locked into a routine of my own doing.

Repeating every day in the same way.

I mean, we know children like routine. I like routine. I was a professional project manager; it was in my DNA! My response to becoming a mum was to become even more organised. This was my way of ensuring that our baby fitted into our lives, being the cherry on our cake.

I didn't want to be one of those mums who was late for stuff because of the baby, so my response was routine. Which, unknowingly, zapped the life out of life. Well, it did for me anyway.

Like all changes in life, we come up with a coping mechanism that works for us. Mine was routine and being organised. For me, it was my default position. I didn't sit down and decide, I just did it. My autopilot naturally took over.

If only I knew then what I know now. Hindsight's a wonderful thing.

It really doesn't have to be this way.

It took me a while to realise what was going on. I initially thought it was because I wasn't happy with my job. But as I've said before, that was just the trigger for looking life in the face and deciding what I really wanted.

I invite you to live more purposefully. To actively choose what the day will bring, how the day will look and what you will do.

The responsibility of how life is for you, sits with you. Why would you give that responsibility to anyone else?

Surely you wouldn't.

So how can you turn it around?

I know that I am at my best when I'm in my flow. Just like water running down the river, I find life easy when I'm in flow. I am able to just get on with things without resistance.

However, life is not always like that.

There are moments when we feel like we are hitting our heads against a brick wall, or pushing against a locked door.

It's at that point that you have a choice to make. You can either keep pushing, which gets you nowhere and leads to frustration. Or you can choose an alternative route.

You can choose the route that best serves you. The route that will actually help you achieve what you want and need.

The thing is, we have so many choices nowadays that it is easy to get confused and be overwhelmed. So instead of choosing what we need and want, we decide to try and do everything. That's when life takes over and we surrender to the treadmill of life.

I know what that feels like, wanting to get involved in everything, being attracted to new projects, just like a magpie is attracted to shiny objects.

It's great to have a full life filled with variety. But not if suddenly you feel like you have no time, or that your time has been hijacked by stuff that you have no interest in. Or that you are unable to spend time doing the things you really want to be doing, with the people who are special to you.

What is the point?

You have the freedom to choose how you spend your time, to really live life.

It's about pausing, reflecting and then choosing your next best action. Knowing yourself as best you can to make the right decision for you.

Over time, we forget who we are, what we want and where we're going. That's why it's good to start with the inner work. Asking simple questions to reacquaint yourself with you. Being able to clearly see what you want, instead of trying to look through the fog of family life and what everyone else wants.

Know what you like

Rather than focusing on the shoulds, coulds, and woulds, put yourself at the top of the list and ask yourself, what do I like? What are the things that put a smile on my face, make my heart sing and put a spring in my step?

It's easy to forget that over time, our lives become merged with others around us, whether it's our partners, children, family or friends. But we are all unique and have our own wants and needs. So dig deep, remember what they are.

Then bring more of that into your life.

Know your strengths

Rather than focusing on what you can't do, focus on what you can do. All the things you're good at, the things you find easy, the things that you don't really have to think about, the things you can do quickly.

Remember, these are our superpowers. Others refer to them as our gifts. You will have many strengths; it's about acknowledging what they are and then doing something with them.

Say no

Rather than trying to please everyone or be everything to everyone, learn to be selective. I know I've said say yes and then figure out the how, but that doesn't mean saying yes to everything just because you can.

It's okay to say no. There are things in life that we don't want to do. It's not personal to whoever is receiving the no, it's just about what's right for you. Your priority is to serve yourself before others.

Ask for help

I used to be terrible at asking for help. Why would I need help when I know I am capable? Then I realised it wasn't about proving how capable I was. Sometimes it's just about accepting help to lighten the load.

Rather than trying to do everything because you can, share the load. Asking for help is not a sign of weakness. It's not about whether you're capable or not. Asking for help is the intelligent thing to do. You don't have to do everything, so ask for help.

Be ready to learn

Rather than accepting what you know, get curious. Be open to new ideas. Ask why. Become intrigued. Learning doesn't stop once we finish our education, it is something that should continue throughout our life. The world is continually changing and there is always something new to learn. Plus, it makes life interesting.

You might want to learn a new skill. You may decide to start a new hobby. You may want to develop a talent you have. Whatever it is, it's your choice what you do next.

The decision to sleepwalk through life, to always be on autopilot and to feel numb to what is going on is yours. Yes, there may be challenges, but the way you think, respond and speak is within your control.

NOW IT'S YOUR TURN

Answer these questions using the following lined pages:

1. Where are you right now?

2. What would be your next best move?

3. How will you make your time count?

4. Are you scared to be seen?

WHY DO YOU FEEL INVISIBLE?

"A star does not compete with other stars around it; it just shines."

Matshona Dhliwayo

I don't know about you, but it seems like everyone is always rushing. Rushing to keep up. Rushing to get something done. Rushing from one thing to another.

And if it's not rushing, it feels more like just being busy, especially if you're a mum.

Too busy looking after everyone else?

Too busy working your way through your to-do list?

Too busy surviving?

I used to love being busy. I thought if I was busy then I was being productive. The thought of just sitting doing nothing was completely alien to me. For as long as I can remember, I've always been busy. I've always filled my time with doing stuff.

Busy getting involved with stuff.

This was all fine before having children because my busyness was more selective. My time and energy were focused on what I wanted. Instinctively, I knew what was best for me.

However, being a mum is a whole different ball game. It's easier to be busy because there's always stuff that needs to be done. And obviously, mums are the ones that should be doing all these extra things! Besides, our partners wouldn't do it how we'd want it done, so we just do it.

That was my thinking but it's not the truth.

You're too busy because you've chosen to be too busy. I know, shock, horror! But it's true. Every day we are presented with a choice. Every day it's up to us to decide what happens next.

Making the decision on what you do next is about awareness. It's about being present. It's about living consciously. However, sometimes it feels easier just to keep going instead of stopping. Instead of making the decision to change and saying yes to you.

The thing is, you're actually just hiding. You've made the decision to be invisible. Being busy just makes it feel legitimate.

So ask yourself, what's your truth?

Do you know who you are?

Do you stand tall and seize every day?

Do you look forward to what opportunities may come your way?

Or have you lost yourself?

Do you not know who you are anymore?

Are you living on autopilot?

It is up to us to ensure that we are fit, healthy and our needs are being met. However, as mums we focus all our energy on others and forget about the most important person in our lives: ourselves.

If you are exhausted and tired, if you haven't the time for you, if you are not at your best, then how can you be the best for others? The answer is you can't.

There is only so long you can continue on this path before you've had enough. Then what would you do?

The good news is, it doesn't have to be like this. You can rediscover who you are and step into being proud of who you are and go after what you want. It just means making a commitment to yourself to put yourself first occasionally.

So why not try the following:

Take yourself out for a catch up

If we're not careful, over time we forget who we are. We've spent so long being Mum that we've forgotten we're also an individual and we do have our own identity. So, start by getting to know who you are and what you want. Take the time to remember all the things that you love about life. Go on a date with yourself.

Take yourself out for a cup of coffee, lunch or just go for a walk.

Me-time

Make time for you. I know I've said this before, but I know I need to repeat myself to get my point across.

You are the most important person in your life. It's true. So give yourself time each day that is just for you. You are more than worth it and you deserve it. Even if it means getting up a little bit earlier to enjoy a cup of something.

Self-care

It's your responsibility to ensure that you are at your best and the way to do that is by caring for yourself. Find out what that is for you and build it into your daily routine. Make it easy so you naturally do it as part of your routine.

Find your inner cheerleader

If you haven't got the message before then here is your reminder. Know how amazing you are and replace that inner critic with your inner cheerleader. Acknowledge everything that is awesome about you and remind yourself regularly. The more you practice, the quicker you will realise this to be true.

It's your responsibility to be the first one to say well done whenever anything goes right and ask how can I do things differently when things don't turn out how you hoped.

Take action

Reflection is great, but it's even better when you then take action. Decide what you want and take small steps to get there. Small steps make it easy. The easier it is for you to start, the more likely you will keep going and the quicker you will progress.

You don't have to continue to be invisible in your life. It's your choice if you want to just blend in. But ultimately will this make you happy or will it leave you with regrets? You can decide what's next. You make the decision on what your next best move is.

NOW IT'S YOUR TURN

Answer these questions using the following lined pages:

1. Are you ready to step into the light?

2. What will it take to become visible?

3. How can you change what you focus on?

4. What does your reality look like

DO YOU NEED
GLASSES?

"Life is about perspective and how you look at something...ultimately, you have to zoom out."

Whitney Wolfe Herd.

It's easy to take things personally. To take offence when someone disagrees with you. To be upset if things don't go your way.

But what if you viewed things differently? What if you were able to have a wider perspective?

During our lifetime, I think we develop tunnel vision.

Let me explain.

How we view the world and how we respond is influenced by our experience of life.

As a mum, I have become more aware of the dangers that exist for my children.

As a business owner, I have become more aware of the challenges that exist in running a business.

As a woman, I have become more aware of the inequalities that exist

191

between men and women.

All of this contributes to how I view different situations and the opinion I now have. It means I focus on certain things.

But that is my view and my opinion. It is not the only view or the only opinion.

By acknowledging that many different perspectives exist — and there can be more than one right answer — life feels easier and less resistant. Life can flow.

The lens through which we see life is determined by many things. It's the roles you play. It's the experiences you have. It's the people you meet.

All these things go into making up our bespoke view of life. It's this lens view that then influences the way we behave, think and speak.

It's an automatic thing.

But it doesn't have to be.

If we take the time to pause and reflect, to become more self-aware, we will see that we have a choice.

We can change that lens so that it serves us instead of it controlling us.

I don't have to tell you that life is full of ups and downs, of twists and turns. Some people seem to manage this with ease. Others, not so well.

Wouldn't it be great if we could accept the rollercoaster of life, knowing that we can handle anything that life throws our way in a calm and measured way? That we're not reacting because of the lens that is in front of us.

For me, that can only start with ourselves and being comfortable with who we are. By having a strong core, truly knowing who we are and seeing life through the lens that we've chosen. But how do you do that?

Values

It starts with understanding what your values are and knowing what values are important to you. Knowing your values helps you to make decisions and take action. When we make a decision or take action that is in alignment with our values, life flows in the right way for us. Life becomes easy.

Perspective

Everyone has their own perspective. That's because everyone is unique. Your point of view could be the polar opposite of the person in front of you. So next time you're talking to someone, acknowledge that their starting point might be different from yours. It will be a different conversation and could even have a happy ending.

Pause, reflect and respond

The outcome of a conversation will be very different if you can pause, reflect and then respond. This momentary break will lessen the emotion and give you time to respond more calmly, as opposed to reacting and then maybe wanting to backtrack.

Reconnect

We are constantly changing and it's easy to not recognise who we have become. Take the time to reconnect with who you really are. What do you like? What makes you laugh? What are you about?

Self-awareness

Being aware of who we are and, more importantly, the impact we have on others is so important in life. It's the difference between living in harmony and potential chaos.

Rather than accepting how you see life, get curious. Understand whether that's really how you see life or if you have adopted someone else's perspective that is just not right for you. More importantly, acknowledge that there are many different perspectives in the world, some of which you can easily appreciate and others that may take you longer.

Just remember to pause, reflect and then respond.

NOW IT'S YOUR TURN

Answer these questions using the following lined pages:

1. How do you see life at the moment?
2. Why is that?
3. What would need to change for you to see things differently?
4. Does life feel hard right now?

LIFE DOESN'T HAVE TO BE HARD

"You only live once, but if you do it right, once is enough."

Mae West

When I look back on my life when I'm old, grey and wrinkly, I want to look back and know my life was easy. Yes, I will have had struggles. Yes, I will have had painful moments. Yes, I will have dealt with challenges. But why does that have to be hard? I have a choice.

A choice on how I deal with those times. How I respond. How I behave. How I speak.

Making life easy, for me, means cutting out all the noise that naturally makes life feel harder. Instead, I choose to be open-minded, to be curious and to be me.

The brain follows the path of least resistance, which implies life will be easy. And it is easy. But at whose expense? Usually yours. How?

Sometimes it's easier to stay quiet rather than use your voice to say how you feel. Sometimes it's just easier to do what someone's asked rather than being curious and asking why. Sometimes it's just easier to go along with the majority, rather than standing alone and doing what you believe to be right for you.

But how does that actually make you feel? Undervalued? Invisible? Unappreciated?

As a busy working mum, it's easy to get stuck doing the mummy juggle. Is that because everything needs to be done? Doing everything for everyone? Trying to be everything for everyone? Just trying to do everything?

And how does that feel? Tiring? Stressful? Frustrating?

What would happen if you stopped juggling? What if you lived your life with more purpose?

What if you could just be?

You'd feel calmer. You'd enjoy the moments. You'd be really living.

The truth is, constantly juggling and managing the busy life of a parent is hard work. But it doesn't have to be. We decide to take on all this stuff, when actually half of it is probably unnecessary and the other half can be shared with others.

I want to help you to live an easier life. A life where you feature as you, not as a mum, sister, friend, auntie or all the other roles you insist on being. Let me help you to get started.

Set healthy boundaries

Having healthy boundaries makes you decide how you'd like to be treated but it also means you can then tell others how you'd like to be treated, what is acceptable and what isn't. It's not about creating barriers between you and everyone else, it's about protecting your space and time so you can be the best you can be.

Focus on what is essential and important

It's easy to want to do everything but is that necessary? It's about being honest about what you do and knowing that everything you do is worth doing.

As I've said before, I'm great at being busy because I see it as being productive. But life is not about being productive. Life is about living. It's about making choices and having the time to focus on what's essential and important instead of saying yes to everyone and everything.

Do one thing at one time

I've said this many times already, juggling may seem like an amazing skill, which it is if you're a juggler! In the real world, focusing properly on more than one thing at one time is actually not possible. The brain can't do it. You will get further and be less stressed if you just do one thing at a time.

So give yourself a break. Do one thing at one time and see how that feels.

Me-time

You know how important I think me-time is. Why wouldn't I? You are the lead actor in your life, so if you're not giving yourself some time and space to just do what you want then you've demoted yourself to a supporting role. Is that what you want? Is that all you deserve?

Do things that make you laugh and smile

Life is about having fun. So do things that put a smile on your face. And you know that one of the best places to get some inspiration is to reflect on your childhood for a clue. If that doesn't help, then ask a child. They may not know the answer but hearing their opinion will make you smile.

Life is what we make it, so if we choose to we can make it hard. However, wouldn't it feel better if we decided to make it easier?

NOW IT'S YOUR TURN

Answer these questions using the following lined pages:

1. Does life feel hard at the moment?

2. What could you do to make it feel easier?

3. How could you change the way you view life to lighten the load?

4. Do you need to become unstuck?

5 REASONS WHY YOU FEEL STUCK

"It always seems impossible until it is done."

Nelson Mandella

Do you wake up and think, 'Is this it?'

Do you feel like you're just coasting through life?

Do you find yourself switching to autopilot the moment you get up?

If you answered yes, then what you're actually experiencing is being stuck. You've surrendered yourself to whatever will be, will be.

How does that feel?

Does this bring you joy, love and happiness?

I doubt it.

The hard truth is, the only reason you're stuck is because you want to be stuck.

The good news is, we all get stuck in life at some point. For some people, it's temporary. For others, it feels like a lifetime. It's not a nice feeling either way. Feeling like there is no way out, like life is just happening to you. Feeling helpless.

The thing is, life is for living not for just existing. It's up to us what happens. It's up to us how our story plays out. It's simply up to us.

Shocking!

But why might you be stuck?

Is it because you think you're too tired?

Is it because you don't have time?

Is it because you're too busy?

Whatever the reason, I just want you to know that you have the power to change things. And more importantly, you are the only one who can change things. No one is going to come and save you. You are responsible for saving yourself.

That's right. It all starts with you.

Yet I have clients who have given up. Who are allowing themselves to get swept away with whatever comes their way and then they wonder why they are not happy.

So why do we feel stuck?

Too tired

You just simply feel tired all the time. Exhausted from life. You find yourself looking at others, family and friends, and you feel envious. You wonder why they don't feel tired too. Their life seems similar to yours, yet they don't appear to be as tired as you. You find yourself thinking, if only I wasn't so tired I'd do something.

You are only tired because you choose to be tired. Like with anything in life, it's the meaning we give to it that gives it power. Look at it this way, children never seem tired. That's because they see life differently than us. They are excited about what might happen. What they might get involved with. And so, they literally go on until their bodies say enough.

Not enough time

You haven't got time to breathe, let alone think about what you want. If only you had more time. If only time didn't fly by. If only, if only, if only.

The only reason there is not enough time is because you've decided there's not enough time and that's what you're telling yourself. If you tell yourself there is not enough time, then guess what? Life will always feel like you don't have enough time. However, your time is yours. It's up to you how you spend it.

Instead of thinking there is not enough time, decide on how you want to spend your time and focus on that.

So, how would you like to spend it?

Too busy

You're stuck on the treadmill of life and locked into your daily routine. This may be true but how did you get here? We don't start life off being busy, we allow ourselves to get busy. It is then up to us to become less busy, to focus on what is important and let everything else go.

I invite you to stop doing the stuff that is 'unnecessary' and start doing the stuff that is 'necessary'. The things that really matter.

Feeling lost

You don't know what you want. You don't know where you are and you don't know where you want to go. Is this true? Do you really not know what you want? Or are you just scared to voice what you want? Are you scared to admit what you want?

The only way to stop feeling lost is to look within yourself and to accept that you have the answer within. Trust me when I say, you do know what you want.

You think this is it

You believe you've created your life, no matter that it doesn't suit you, and so you just need to carry on. The fact is, it's never too late. You always have the choice to change the direction of the path you're on. To make decisions that best serve you. Remember, you get to decide what happens next every time you wake up.

Whatever your reason, I want you to know that all it takes to change is you. Decide that this is not where you want to be, that it's time to change and take the first step.

NOW IT'S YOUR TURN

Answer these questions using the following lined pages:

1. Why do you feel stuck?
2. What can you do to change things?
3. What will motivate you to do something different?
4. Are you relying on some luck to change things?

THERE'S NO SUCH THING AS GOOD LUCK

"Luck can only get you so far."

J. K. Rowling

My husband is fed up with me correcting him when he says we're lucky. As far as I'm concerned, it's got nothing to do with luck. Worse than that, saying we're lucky, for me, totally disregards our efforts that have got us to where we are today. That's why I get really frustrated when I hear people talking about how lucky they are or how lucky someone else is.

The truth is, people are not 'lucky'. It's not about chance. It's about having the drive to make things happen. It's not about waiting for someone to wave a magic wand. It's not about waiting to be in the right place at the right time. It's not about waiting for someone else to make your dreams come true.

It's easy to sit back and just let life happen. It takes no effort. You don't have to think. When it all goes wrong, you can blame someone else.

The thing is, we are all responsible for the actions we take or, in this case, don't take. By doing nothing, you've still made a decision. Whether you agree or not, you've still decided to do nothing. Therefore, whatever happens next is a consequence of you deciding to do nothing. So you can't blame someone else.

That's why I say, there's no such thing as luck. It's all about attitude. It's all about how we see life. It's all about perspective.

Think of it this way: how would you feel if someone saw your progress as you being lucky? Wouldn't that devalue your hard work? Similarly, doesn't saying someone's unlucky make their inaction more legitimate?

If you want things to be different, stop waiting for good luck to come your way and go make it happen.

If it's not luck, what is it?

Positive attitude

This may seem simple but it's true. Being positive, having a positive outlook on life, looking for the positives all make such a difference and is so powerful in influencing the results we get.

If you sit in a negative space, then all you will see is the negative.

Now I'm not suggesting that you need to be Little Miss Sunshine every day. Life is full of ups and downs, of twists and turns. It's just deciding not to dwell on challenges.

If you choose to sit in the positive, you will be amazed at what happens. You'll see opportunities coming your way. You'll be able to move forward with ease. Everything will seem a lot clearer.

Inner cheerleader

You know I'm all about being comfortable with yourself. Instead of relying on others to lift you up, I will always encourage you to start on the inside. Nurture your inner cheerleader, which takes continual practice. And just like a muscle, the more we practise and train ourselves the easier this will be.

It's about knowing you can, then believing you can, then taking action to show that you can.

Having direction

Know what you want and what you need. You may think you don't know but let me tell you, you do. We all do. It's just about letting it out.

Once you realise what it is, this is what will stop you from just going around in circles.

Taking action

Starting is the most difficult part, so it's about taking things one step at a time. It's all about taking that first step, no matter the size, otherwise you'll just stay stuck.

Having a tribe

Have people around you who are your supporters. It's not about surrounding yourself with the 'yes' crowd, it's about surrounding yourself with individuals who genuinely want you to succeed and will be honest with you.

It's got nothing to do with luck. It's about you. The decisions you make and the actions you take. You will only get to where you want to go if you decide you're going to get there.

NOW IT'S YOUR TURN

Answer these questions using the following lined pages:

1. What will help you to move forward?
2. What do you need to do to progress?
3. What will you focus on?

MULTITASKING IS NOTHING TO BE PROUD OF

"Concentrate all your thoughts upon the work at hand. The sun's rays do not burn until brought to a focus."

Alexander Graham Bell

We're busy, busy, busy, trying to do 101 things. We're so busy that we try and do things simultaneously, so that we can tick more things off our to-do list, which seems never ending.

What if we stopped being so busy?

What if we focused on what was important?

What if we tried to do one thing at one time?

Wouldn't life feel calmer? Wouldn't we be happier? Wouldn't we be living in the here and now?

Confession time, although you already know this, I was a serial multitasker. I'm quite good at it. In fact, I'm proud of the fact that I can multitask. I love ticking things off my to-do list and being able to do tasks simultaneously, or that's what I thought.

The thing is, multitasking is not as good as we think it is. Trying to multitask is stressful, puts us under unnecessary pressure and stops us from being present.

If we just learnt to do one thing at one time, we'd get a lot more done, we'd be calmer and less stressed.

As women, we're known to have the amazing ability to multitask. The ability to juggle lots of balls at once. It sounds like an amazing skill to have. After all, we get lots done. But, is it really that good and what is the cost?

The truth is, just because we can doesn't mean we should. Multitasking has its benefits, but it's not as great as we think it is.

The interesting thing to consider is why do we do it? We see a job and think it has to be done as nobody else will do it. We decide we must take it on! But is this true? Is this the reality we want for ourselves?

We get stressed because we are trying to juggle too much. We make mistakes because we're doing too much. It takes us longer because we're doing too much.

Just consider how life would be better if we did one thing at one time.

Calmer

Think about how stressed you get when you're trying to do lots of things all at once. For me, it was usually trying to cook, whilst getting school uniforms ready for the next day. Trying to appease my children and answering an important phone call!

However, I've found that I feel calmer if I just pay attention to one thing at one time. After all, spinning one plate is less stressful than spinning three.

Focus

In reality, we cannot actually focus on more than one thing so why do we try? Just think about it, when you try to do more than one thing at a time, are you really paying full attention to all of them? Or are you trying to divide your attention — which is impossible!

I realise I have limitations and the ability to focus, properly, on more than one thing at a time is not possible. So I'm practising focusing on just one thing at a time and I can honestly say life is a lot easier.

More productive

It's true, we're actually more productive by doing one thing at one time instead of trying to do many things all at once! Try it and see what happens. Because I'm giving my undivided attention to just one activity, I get it done in a shorter amount of time which means I can move onto the next more quickly.

Fewer mistakes

I don't know about you, but if I'm trying to do too much at once, I definitely tend to make more mistakes. This goes back to trying to divide my attention, it's not possible. So ultimately, I make mistakes. They may be small, but sometimes it also means having to redo stuff. This means not only has it ultimately taken me longer, but the first time was a waste of my precious effort.

Complete tasks

By trying to do a lot at once, we risk not completing what we started. This is because we're interrupting ourselves or distracting ourselves with other tasks, so we have to reset ourselves constantly when moving from task to task. There have been times when I've actually had to start again because I've forgotten where I stopped and it's easier just to go back to the beginning. Another waste of time and effort.

Although being able to multitask is an impressive skill to have, it comes at a price. It is up to you whether you continue to pay that price or decide to focus on one thing at one time.

NOW IT'S YOUR TURN

Answer these questions using the following lined pages:

1. What do you need to stop doing?
2. How can you take the pressure off?
3. Who do you need help from?

DO YOU SUFFER FROM COMPARISONITIS?

"The only person you should try to be better than is who you were yesterday."

Unknown

It's very common to compare yourself to those around you. We all do it. For you, it might be what you look like, how well you're doing in your career or how good you are as a mother.

But why? What is the point? How is it helpful?

The truth is, it's pointless, not helpful and a waste of energy.

As individuals we are all unique. We all have our own path to follow. We all have different wants and needs. Everyone's history is different.

This means that comparing yourself to another is a waste of time. You're not comparing like with like. More like apples with oranges, both are fruit but different from one another.

The thing is, we seem to enjoy dwelling in the 'lack' of our lives, which comparing helps us see, and this makes it difficult to acknowledge the abundance in our lives and how amazing we are.

Let's look at it in a different way. How often do you give yourself a compliment? Never, sometimes, or every day? Maybe you're thinking, 'Why would I give myself a compliment?'

I've said it before and I'll say it again: it is your responsibility to be your own cheerleader. To be the first one to say how great you are and to shout from the rooftops why you're amazing. Even if it isn't considered the 'done thing'!

It's about changing your focus to help cure you of comparisonitis, so you stop looking to the outside world and instead bring the focus back to you.

External validation is nice, but the only opinion about you that counts is your own. Why wait for someone else to say, 'Well done!', or, 'Great job!' or, 'You look great!', when you can say it to yourself whenever you want.

So how can we stop? It's all about getting to know, like and appreciate how amazing you actually are.

Practice gratitude

Make a list of all the things that you are grateful for in your life, no matter the size or value. When you start focusing on what you have to be grateful for, you will see all the amazing things that are already present in your life.

Acknowledge your achievements

Make a list of everything you have achieved, no matter the size or value. To get this far you have already achieved a lot and each and every item on your list is worth celebrating.

You have many strengths

Make a list of all your strengths. All the things you know you can do. You have many, but you may have forgotten what they are. There's so much you can do with the strengths you have, the potential that you could unlock instead of keeping yourself stuck.

Know you're great

Make a list of all the reasons why you're great. Yes, you are great and you need to know and acknowledge why. Not only will this give you inner confidence, but also a solid foundation to know that you can achieve anything.

Have many wishes

Make a list of all of your wishes and then take action to make them come true. Rather than comparing yourself to others, go make your own dreams come true. Inspire others, by your actions, to do the same.

The good news is you have the power to stop comparing yourself with others. You do this by replacing it with something even better. Instead, start to love who you are, where you've come from and where you want to go.

When you realise how wonderful you truly are, you will notice how the external world will change for you, you will view life differently and great things will happen.

NOW IT'S YOUR TURN

Answer these questions using the following lined pages:

1. Why do you compare yourself to others?

2. How does it make you feel?

3. What would stop you from comparing yourself?

4. What do you need to do to feel confident in your abilities?

5. How can you break your comparisonitis habit?

A BAD HABIT IS SO
⟆ MUCH EASIER ⟆

"Motivation is what gets you started. Habit is what keeps you going."

Jim Rohn

I don't need to tell you that a habit is something we do automatically. It's something that we do without thinking and it's something that can happen subconsciously.

Good or bad, we all have habits. There are ones we like and ones we want to change. Good or bad, the choice is ours.

If we want to change a habit, we can. The power to do something differently is ours. The question is, do you want to change? Are you willing to practice? Are you willing to practice for as long as it takes until you form a new habit?

Or will you choose to fall at the first hurdle? Will you give up when it gets too hard? Will you stop when you lose interest?

The choice is yours.

Let's keep this really simple. Changing habits, which are truly embedded, is not easy. It takes effort. It takes practice. It takes commitment. But there are steps you can take to make your life easier and to help you change.

Make small changes

It's much easier to start if that first step is easy and that means making it small. By focusing on taking one small step at a time, as opposed to a giant leap that can be too big and scary, you'll make immediate progress. Say you want to write a book. Writing just one page or 100 words a day feels easier than setting time aside to write the whole book. Or what if you want to run a marathon? Building up to it by running short distances to start with feels more manageable than trying to run a marathon on day one.

Small changes are easier to complete and so you stay motivated to keep going. Whereas trying to make a major shift will be a lot more difficult and you're more likely to feel disheartened if you go wrong.

Reward yourself regularly

It's important to reward ourselves regularly. One of the reasons we continue with bad habits is that we are getting immediate satisfaction, something that we crave. However, when we're trying to form a new habit the 'satisfaction' takes a while to materialise. Without this satisfaction, we start to get turned off and it starts to lose its appeal.

The answer: rewarding ourselves regularly. It's a motivator. It also reinforces the message that we're progressing and that we're doing well.

Repeat, repeat and repeat again

Forming a new habit takes repetition. Daily repetition is good, but repetition many times in a day is even better. The more we repeat a new behaviour, the quicker it will become a habit.

Just notice some of the habits you'll do as part of your everyday routine, like brushing your teeth. You don't think about doing it, you just do it. This is because it's something you do every day.

Make it easy

We know that change can be difficult, so the key is to make it easier. Think of what you could do to make it easier for yourself to form a new habit. If you want to start eating more fruit, place a fruit bowl somewhere where you see it all the time during the day. Don't hide it in the kitchen, place it in view. If you want to drink more water, carry a water bottle with you.

Remove any obstacles

Another step to making things easier is to remove any obstacles that might stop you. Think of all the reasons that will stop you from practising your new behaviour, then remove them. If you want to go for a run in the morning, have your clothes ready the night before so you can just go. If you hate your feet getting wet when you're running, buy some waterproof trainers.

So you see, there are some simple things you can do to help you form a new habit or change a behaviour. By applying small and simple techniques, you're more likely to change. This is because they are achievable and so we feel like we're winning. If we feel like we're winning then we'll stay motivated and we're more likely to keep going.

NOW IT'S YOUR TURN

Answer these questions using the following lined pages:

1. What would help you to get started?

2. How can you make changing easier?

3. What would give you the confidence to make a change?

YOU DON'T HAVE TO BE LOUD
TO BE CONFIDENT

"The most beautiful thing you can wear is confidence."

Blake Lively

We all have our own idea of what confidence looks like. It might be being able to easily walk into a room full of strangers, or being able to easily speak in front of a packed room. It might be being able to easily speak your mind when you know it's different from the majority.

But what does it take to be able to do all these things?

You may say someone who appears to be an extrovert, who is doing all the talking and who's comfortable being in the presence of strangers.

Is this person confident?

Do you know what they might be thinking whilst seemingly projecting a confident person? They may actually be really self-conscious and being loud and vocal is their coping mechanism for this.

Similarly, do you assume that a quiet person lacks confidence?

We can't assume the loud person in the room, who is easily able to hold court, is confident whilst the quiet person in the crowd lacks confidence.

For me, confidence comes from within. It's not what you're projecting. It's about being comfortable in your own skin. It's about being comfortable with who you are and knowing you are okay exactly as you are.

In my opinion, we spend far too much time focusing on what others think of us, rather than being happy with what we think of ourselves. And I mean honestly content with how amazing we are. Because if we're content on the inside, if we're strong on the inside, we'll have developed a powerful inner confidence that will mean we're in a better place to deal with whatever life throws at us.

It's simple; what really matters is what you think. That's what will make you confident.

Fake it until you make it

To start with, it is about faking it until you make it and embodying the traits of people you view as confident. It's about striking that superman pose to tell yourself that you are confident.

Change the story

If you keep telling yourself you're not confident then don't be surprised at the lack of confidence you have. If you want to be confident, tell yourself you are until you truly believe it.

Stop listening to your inner critic

As I've said before, our inner voice is neither good nor bad, it's about protecting the species. The thoughts that pop into our heads are about keeping us safe. Keeping us in our comfort zone. If you want to grow in confidence, get out of your comfort zone. Your confidence will grow the more you test your boundaries and experience new things.

Focus on the positive

It's easy to say, but focus on the good rather than dwelling on the bad. When you focus on the negative, your body starts to take on the posture of someone who wants to hide away. Instead, focus on the positive and then notice how you stand tall, you hold your head up and you walk more assertively.

Become comfortable in yourself

The most important thing is to be comfortable with who you are. It's that inner confidence that really matters. Be aware of all the wonderful things that you have to offer and use this to grow your inner confidence.

Confidence is like a muscle, you need to continuously be working it because over time, just like a muscle, if you don't work it you may find that your confidence fades and you won't even realise it.

NOW IT'S YOUR TURN

Answer these questions using the following lined pages:

1. What's stopping you from being confident?
2. What do you need to do to overcome this?
3. What would help you to become more confident?
4. What would help you to enjoy being confident?

DADS
HAVE MORE FUN

"You can't reach for anything new if your hands are still full of yesterday's junk."

Louise Smith

Dads have more fun because they focus on having fun instead of the 101 things that mums think have to be done before the fun can happen!

When I first became a mum, my main focus was on ensuring that I kept my baby safe. Was she dressed appropriately? Was I feeding her enough? Was her environment safe? I was a worrier, I was her protector. If anything bad happened to her, it would be my fault.

Whereas my husband was more relaxed. He had the same concerns but he seemed to be enjoying having her in our life.

This didn't really change when we had our son. In fact, I probably got a little worse, especially when he caught Bronchiolitis, which meant a week's stay in the hospital when he was just 3 weeks old.

But over time, I realised that if I wanted things to change, if I wanted to have fun with my children, I needed to change. Not so easy when you're a project manager; a professional organiser!

But it's simply a matter of perspective and priority. It's a matter of what's important.

So instead of wondering why dads have more fun, decide what is important to you, make that your priority and then make it happen.

Just because he's Fun Dad doesn't mean you can't be Fun Mum.

It's all about choice. Rather than dwelling on why he's Fun Dad, choose to be Fun Mum.

We are in control of what we think, say and do. So being Fun Mum is all about changing the way we think, what we say and what we do.

Here are five things to think about that will get you started:

Importance

Decide what is important to you. Obviously, there are chores that need to be done, some of which are important. But not everything that we fill our day with is important. Plus we really don't have to do everything ourselves. We do have options. We can ask for help.

Prioritise

If you know what is important you can then decide what is your priority. This may sound clinical but it really isn't. If you want to have fun, then it has to be your priority. As long as you know your children are clothed and fed, the rest can wait.

Top tip: agree on some boundaries as a family so that everyone has time to do their 'boring stuff'.

Focus on one thing

Men are better at this than us women. We insist on juggling which, as I've said before, is a waste of effort. Being a fun mum is much easier if you're fully present with your children rather than trying to multitask!

Judgement

We worry too much about what everyone else thinks, rather than what we think. We know what is best for ourselves and our family and that's what matters. It's about trusting your instinct rather than dwelling on what is right or wrong according to Freda The Supermum!

Go with the flow

Let it go and go with the flow. I love a plan and routine, but having fun cannot be planned or scheduled. It happens when you dare to let go. Just go with whatever is happening, without the drama of organising and making sure everything is just so.

Over time I have learnt to let go and relax a little. Not just by watching my husband and following his lead, but also because it's hard work keeping everything going and life shouldn't be like that. I want to enjoy life.

I want to live life to its fullest. It's about having balance and balancing. If you focus on what's really important, rather than what needs to be done, it's much easier.

NOW IT'S YOUR TURN

Answer these questions using the following lined pages:

1. What's distracting you from having fun?
2. What could you do to remove these distractions?
3. What is fun for you?

AND FINALLY

"The most effective way to do it, is to do it."

Amelia Earhart

Congratulations on getting to the end of the book! I hope you have found it useful and it has inspired you to make life happen instead of letting life happen to you.

I would like to leave you with one final story to end this book.

I'd like to introduce you to a very special little girl. Someone who is feisty, fearless and believes anything is possible. If you tell her something cannot be done then she will show you it can. If you tell her she's unable to do something then she will show you she's more than capable. If you tell her she's not good enough then she'll show you she's more than good enough.

Who is this little girl? Meet young Maria. Yes, that's right. Meet my child self.

When I was young I truly believed that nothing was going to hold me back. It fired me up when someone told me I wouldn't be able to do this or I'd never be able to do that. I basked in the glory of proving people wrong, especially if it was something I was particularly passionate about.

My first memory of this, that stands out, is when my maths teacher told me I wouldn't get an A in maths GCSE. I was crushed. I loved maths. It was my favourite subject. The thought of not getting an A was devastating. I swore then and there I would get an A. Guess what? I got an A.

Next was one of the Guide Leader Assistants who told me I'd never be a Patrol Leader. I know some of you will have no idea what that is. It's the leader of a troop within a Guiding group. I couldn't quite understand why she'd say something like that. It was my dad who reminded me that I was good enough and more than capable. So I made it happen, I became a Patrol Leader.

And finally, a family member told me I wouldn't be as successful as my brother. I remember thinking the cheek of it. How dare he make assumptions. Who does he think is he? I'll show you! Well, I had a very successful 17 year career in Rolls-Royce and now I'm taking that success and building my own business.

When I was younger, I was alive. I was tenacious. I was stubborn. I was focused. I was driven. I knew what I wanted.

I see that same spirit in my daughter and my son. They're both amazing.

I love how they both want to have a go. I love that they're little performers. I love that they wear their hearts on their sleeves. They challenge me. They make life interesting. They make me laugh. They make me beam with pride. They make me want to give them a big hug and never let go.

I don't want them to change. I want them to keep being themselves, whatever that means. I don't want them to be influenced by the negativity in this world. By the judgement. By the conformists. I want them to continue to be brave. I want them to have the courage to say yes when they want to; and also no.

Over the years, I toned down some of those qualities that made me, me. I became a little quieter. I was less flamboyant. I was less likely to rock the boat. I was more likely to conform.

My actions became more considered. Subconsciously, I'd do a quick risk assessment before I attempted something. I was no longer 'gung-ho' about things. I was less likely to jump in with both feet regardless of the impact.

But things have changed. I've changed. Every day I work on becoming the best I can be.

Don't get me wrong. I'm never going to do something that is actually dangerous. Like jumping out of an aeroplane. Or doing a bungee jump. Or swimming with sharks. That's just not my thing. But there are plenty of opportunities that don't mean risking my life.

I've already done one; I've started my own business.

Becoming a mum has definitely changed things for me personally. It's woken me up, although not at first. To begin with, like most mums, I was in survival mode. Learning to take care of my baby, who was totally dependent on me. I was immersed in being a good mum. I had no time or energy for anything else.

But then I made the decision that changed my life. You know the one. I left my corporate career. That was the start of this awesome journey that I am now on.

Because of that one decision, I have been able to experience life as I never thought it could be.

I pinch myself when I look back at how far I've come.

Creating and living the life you want never stops. It's a continuous adventure. It's full of ups and downs and twists and turns.

I have pushed myself out of my comfort zone and said yes to many things I've never done before. For me, life is an adventure, which means saying yes to interesting things.

This is your moment to decide what is next. What is your best next move? Are you ready to make the most of life and seek out the opportunities that will make your journey the best it can be, or will you choose to sit back, relax and chill?

You decide.

"Remember, every day is an opportunity to do something different and if it feels too hard, just focus on taking the first small step."

Maria Andreas Newman

ABOUT THE AUTHOR

Maria grew up in the West Country and now lives in Bristol with her husband and two children.

Maria has many passions in life, many of which support her wellbeing. She believes that anything can be solved by sitting around the dinner table and eating a delicious meal that she's cooked.

She loves being outside and going for a run, not necessarily because she loves running but because she gets time to herself. She gets to listen to an inspiring book on Audible and she can immerse herself in nature. She also enjoys the discipline and physical challenge of kickboxing martial arts, which started because she won a freebie in a Christmas raffle in 2018.

ABOUT MUMMY ON A BREAK

Maria Andreas Newman is otherwise known as Mummy on a Break. She is the founder of The Busy Working Mums Club. She is a coach, mentor and trainer.

Maria knows all too well what it is like to feel stuck and to have challenges in life. Challenges that seem difficult to overcome when you're a busy working mum.

That's why Maria started Mummy on a Break. She took the opportunity to step away from her corporate career, as a project manager working for Rolls-Royce, so that she could focus on what was next.

She'd become caught up on the treadmill of life and found herself waking up most mornings thinking 'is this it?' Having put off doing something about it, she took the brave decision to take action and left her corporate job, which at the time was the thing that was making her feel stuck.

Having been on her own journey to become unstuck, Maria now helps corporate mums to overcome their obstacles so they can have a stress free and happy life through 1:1 coaching.

To find out more, come and connect with Maria:

Website: www.mummyonabreak.co.uk

Facebook group:

www.facebook.com/groups/thebusyworkingmumsclub

Facebook page: www.facebook.com/MummyOnABreak

Instagram: www.instagram.com/mummyonabreak

LinkedIn: www.linkedin.com/in/maria-newman/

Podcast: www.anchor.fm/mummyonabreak

Pinterest: www.pinterest.co.uk/mummyonabreakMaria/

YouTube: www.youtube.com/channel/UClEhv_9PngF-jQHiuBI1pkg

WORK WITH MUMMY ON A BREAK

Maria just wants to help you.

As you've read, Maria knows how hard it can be to start something new and to change direction. She may not have walked in your shoes, but she can appreciate the journey that you're about to start.

Let her guide you with compassion and honesty so that you can get to where you want to be. Let her help you take the action that will get you started. Let her help you to help yourself.

Intrigued?

Working with Maria is really easy. She offers 1:1 coaching as well as online interactive workshops.

1:1 coaching

Maria offers two 1:1 coaching programmes. You can either work with her for 6 months, giving you the time and space to dive deep into the areas you want to work on, or for a half day intensive where you can deep dive into a specific topic that you'd like to resolve.

"Maria is so wonderful and has such a natural gift for helping you see past your own limiting beliefs. I recently had a coaching session with her and it was so insightful and helped me understand areas that I need to focus on. She made some amazing suggestions and really helped me think about what I was really stuck on and how to work through it."

Tamsin Broster

"Maria is so great I'm coming for more. I had some limiting beliefs about me and where I stand now I'm a mum to 2 little boys. So many things changed, I'm still looking for the new me. Maria opened my eyes. We started with answering a few questions to establish what we needed to focus on. Her honesty is super refreshing. She'll tell you how it is and you'll feel you've grown many inches. I've made more progress with her in 60 min than with 'specialists' in 4 months."

Yarka Krajickova

To find out how you can work with Maria follow this link: www.mummyonabreak.co.uk/work-with-me/

Workshops

Maria delivers online interactive workshops. If you want to publish a podcast, deliver a workshop or be organised when it comes to social media and blogging then check out which workshops are currently running. We assure you it will be one of the most valuable 60 minutes of your life!

"I attended one of Maria's workshop on podcasting and was super impressed. Not only was the content easy to follow, Maria made a complex subject (well, as I thought at the time!) very straightforward. Maria was full of enthusiasm and encouragement and was a joy to listen to. However, the thing that has really blown me away, is that Maria has continued to stay in touch and check in with my project and how it's going. She has even been kind enough to give me feedback and share her thoughts on my work, all off her own back. I don't think I've ever experienced that kind of personal care and genuine interest after attending any workshop ever. I'd recommend anyone attend a workshop of Maria's. Thank you Maria!"

Laura Summerhayes

To find out more about the workshops Maria delivers follow this link: www.mummyonabreak.co.uk/workshops/

More testimonials

"Great lunchtime workshop to start the week. How could I resist, when it's titled - How to make money from your SUPERPOWER in 5 easy steps. And I am so glad I attended... the fabulous Maria, Mummy on a Break, delivered a very informative talk and gave me some food for thought. Hopefully, I will be able to capitalise on my creative skills, a career in the design industry, and the advice & tips that I have picked up over the years. All I need to do now is follow your 5 easy steps - to success! Where should I start; webinar, workshop, e-learning?"

Mike Land

"I attended Maria A Newman's workshop on the dreaded subjects of social media and blogging - my 2 pet hates.
What a surprise to come away feeling inspired with a made to measure blueprint of what I can do and how I can do it - without learning anything more.
Maria takes the hard work and hype out of the topics with her down to earth approach and zest for living and valuing time!
Totally recommend this workshop when it comes around again.
Thanks Maria A Newman"

Jaz Goven

"I recently attended one of Maria's online taster workshops called "Manage your mind in 5 easy steps". Being prone to overwhelm, this immediately appealed to me - and certainly didn't disappoint. Within the space of an hour, Maria had given us some fantastic tips and tools to manage our monkey brains and combat negative thinking... Tools I have been using ever since and found to be extremely effective with both myself and my son... Thank you Maria!"

Laura Stevens

Printed in Great Britain
by Amazon

79825929R00153